The Conversion of Edith Stein

The Conversion of Edith Stein

Florent Gaboriau

Translation and Preface by
Ralph McInerny

St. Augustine's Press
South Bend, Indiana

Library of Congress Cataloging in Publication Data
Gaboriau, Florent.
    [Lorsque Edith Stein se convertit. English]
    The conversion of Edith Stein / Florent Gaboriau ;
    translation and preface by Ralph McInerny.
       p. cm.
    Includes bibliographical references and index.
    ISBN 1-58731-125-9 (alk. paper)
    1. Stein, Edith, Saint, 1891–1942. 2. Catholic converts –
    Germany – Biography. 3. Christian converts from
    Judaism – Germany – Biography. 4. Discalced Carmelite
    Nuns – Germany – Biography. 5. Christian saints –
    Germany – Biography. I. Title.
BX4700.S74 G3313 2001
282'.092 – dc21   2001004045

The several translations of Edith Stein's works are drawn from
those in the Carmelite edition of her works: *Edith Stein: Collected
Works* (Washington, D.C.: ICS Publications), vol. 1, pp. 215–17;
vol. 2, pp. 118–20; and 4, pp. 15–17 and 109–12.

∞ *The paper used in this publication meets the minimum requirements
of the International Organisation for Standardization (ISO) - Paper
for documents - Requirements for permanence - ISO 9706: 1994.*

Printed in the Czech Republic by Newton Printing Ltd.   www.newtonprinting.com

Christ is both God and man, and anyone who would participate in his life must take part in the divine and in the human. He who belongs to Christ must relive the whole of his life, grow to become his alter ego. He must walk the way of the crucifixion, weep in Gethsemane, climb Calvary. All the sufferings that come from without are as nothing compared with the dark night of the soul when the divine light no longer shines and the voice of the Lord is muted. God is present, but hidden and silent. Why is it so? These are the mysteries of God of which we speak and it is impossible to explain them completely.

Edith Stein
The Science of the Cross

CONTENTS

Preface		ix
Chronology		13
1.	When Edith Stein Converted	20
	Memories of Youth	22
2.	The Conversion of a Jewess	26
	On Woman	32
3.	The Conversion of a Woman	36
	On Death, with reference to Heidegger	46
4.	The Conversion of a Philosopher	50
	On Spiritual Discernment	59
5.	Conversion Extended over Time	62
	The Interior Life	82
6.	Conversion for all?	88
	Christian Philosophy	102
7.	Conversion Achieved	110
	The Hidden Life and the Epiphany	115
8.	The Canonization of Edith Stein	123

PREFACE

In the person of Edith Stein, the history of salvation is recapitulated in the drama of an individual soul. A daughter of Israel who became a Catholic, she saw the New Covenant as the fulfillment of the Old. The "final solution" of the Third Reich did not spare Jews who had become Christians, and when Edith and her sister Rosa were taken from the Carmelite convent in Echt for deportation, she went willingly to die for her people. It is the irony of martyrdom that the victim eclipses his executioner. Hitler and Himmler and Seyss-Inquart recede into the background. Monsters arisen from the dark depths of the human soul, they can seem fantastic and incredible to us now. But the millions who were brutally captured, deported, and gassed become more real by the day. St. Maximilian Kolbe represents the many who achieved holiness in the death camps. In the case of Edith Stein, her abrupt death revealed a life of profound meaning: the pursuit of holiness.

Florent Gaboriau tells the story of Edith Stein's conversion by examining what she was converted *from*. And he shows that hers was in a sense a triple conversion. A Jewess, a feminist, and a philosopher became Catholic, but these antecedents were transformed rather than jettisoned. Gaboriau, whose *Edith Stein, Philosopher*, still untranslated and is one of the few books that casts light on the saint as a philosopher, is a writer deserving of attention from English language readers. It is fitting that his account of the conversion of Edith Stein be the first work of his to be translated into English. It demonstrates the virtues of brevity, gives us an account at once biographical and spiritual, and is seasoned with excerpts from the writings of the saint.

This book was originally published prior to the canonization of Saint Teresa Benedicta of the Cross, Edith Stein, which took place on October 12, 1998. But it was written in the full confidence that she would be enrolled in the calendar of the saints. This English translation includes Pope John Paul II's homily at the canonization Mass and supplements the excerpts chosen by Philibert Secretan for the French edition and adds a chronology.

Canonized saints are set before us because they exhibit an extraordinary mode of living the Christian life. St. Edith Stein has a special role to play in bringing Catholics and Jews closer together. There have been angry reactions to the role she has been chosen to play. For some she is a sign of contradiction, but then so was Jesus. This little book introduces us to the extraordinary woman, brilliant and accomplished, an established philosopher who turned away from her earlier ambitions to concentrate on the one thing needful. In the obscurity of the convent, in the obscure light of faith, in the dark night of the soul, she ascended the mystical Mount Carmel. But it is Calvary and the cross that are at the center of her spiritual life. Along with St. Bridget of Sweden and St. Catherine of Siena, she has been named co-patroness of Europe. She is a saint to intercede for the West as it takes on, more and more, the aspects of a Culture of Death, in John Paul II's phrase. The monsters of the Third Reich may be gone, but the Nazi contempt for "worthless life" has become a constitutional right in countries that once condemned it.

Ralph McInerny

CHRONOLOGY

1891
October 12. Born in Breslau into a devout Jewish family.

1893
July. Death of her father, Siegfried.

1906
Completes Victoria School and then spends 10 months helping her married sister, Else. "I consciously stopped praying."

1907
Is tutored in Latin and Mathematics.

1908–1911
Realgymnasium in Breslau.

1911–1913
Studies at the University of Breslau.

1912
Winter. Teaches beginning English. Summer. Severe depression related to the meaning of life.

1913–1916
Studies at the University of Göttingen.

1913
Interest in religious questions begins. Depression lifts at hearing "A Mighty Fortress Is Our God."

1914
Serves as Red Cross nurse in the hospital of Mährisch-Weisskirchen.

1916
Thesis: *Zum Problem der Einfühlung* (*The Problem of Empathy*), published in 1917.

1917–1919
Assistant of Edmund Husserl at Fribourg.

1917
Ph. D. *summa cum laude*.
November. Adolf Reinach killed in Flanders.

1918
"Encounter with the cross" at the home of Pauline Reinach, whom she helps arrange her husband's papers.

February. resigns her position with Husserl. Unable to be named to a professorship.

1920–1923
Works toward *habilitation* to qualify for faculty position.

1921
Summer. Stays with Theodore and Hedwig Conrad-Martius. Reads St. Teresa of Avila, buys missal and catechism and asks for baptism.

1922
January 1. Baptized at Bergzabern.

1922–1931
Professor with the Dominicans of Saint Magdalen College for Women at Speyer. Recommended by Canon Schwind, her spiritual director.

1925
Erich Pryzwara, S.J., suggests she translate Newman's letters and diaries into German, then Thomas Aquinas. *Eine Untersuchung über die Staat* (*On the State*).

1927

Canon Schwend dies and Abbot Raphael Walzer of Beuron becomes her spiritual director. Advises against becoming a Carmelite and recommends an active life in the world.

1929

"Husserl's Phenomenology and the Philosophy of Saint Thomas Aquinas."

1931

Left Speyer. Begins translating St. Thomas's *Disputed Question on Truth*. Meeting with Heidegger at Freiburg.

1932

Begins to lecture on vocation of woman. Radio addresses.

Teaches at the German Institute of Scientific Pedagogy at Münster (1932–1933).

September, attends the *Journées de Juvisy* devoted to phenomenology.

Translation of Aquinas appears to mixed reviews.

1933

January. Hitler comes to power.

April. Forbidden by Nazis to teach.
May. Abbot Walzer agrees she should enter Carmel.
July. Extern at Carmel for a month.
August. Last visit to her mother.
October 14. Enters the Carmel of Cologne.

1934
April 15. Takes the habit: Sister Teresa Benedicta of the Cross.
Works on *Endliches und ewiges Sein* (*Finite and Eternal Being*).

1936
September 14. Edith's mother dies.

1938
April 21. Perpetual vows.
April 27. Husserl dies.
November 8. *Kristallnacht.*
December 31. Flight to the Carmel at Echt, Holland.

1939
Passion Sunday. Offers herself as "victim for real peace."

1940
Summer. Her sister Rosa arrives at Echt.

1941
Finishes her work on the symbolic theology of Pseudo-Dionysius.
August. Begins *The Science of the Cross*.
Edict requiring deportation of non-Aryan Germans from Holland by December 15. Nuns contact Carmel of Le Paquier in Switzerland for possible transfer of Edith.
September 1. Jews required to wear the Star of David.

1942
July 26. Dutch Bishops issue pastoral on racism and anti-Semitism.
July 27. Reprisal. All Catholic Jews to be deported by week's end.
August 2. Edith and Rosa taken from Echt Carmel by SS to Amersfoort Prison Camp.
August 5. Arrive at Westerbork Concentration Camp; Edith's final message to her community.
August 1. Deported to Auschwitz.

August 9. Death in gas chamber at Auschwitz-Birkenau.

1987
May 1. Beatified as martyr by Pope John Paul II.

1998
October 12. Canonization by John Paul II of Saint Teresa Benedicta of the Cross.

1999
October 1. St. Bridget of Sweden, St. Catherine of Siena, and St. Edith Stein named co-patronesses of Europe.

1

WHEN EDITH STEIN CONVERTED

There can be found at Göttingen a commemorative plaque that reads, *Edith Stein, Philosopher.* But there is nowhere one that reads, *Edith Stein, Convert* – or one that commemorates her as a spiritual person. But should the curiosity that philosophers have for the former, even granted the uncommon itinerary of her thought, entirely eclipse the much greater interest of her passage to Christianity when she became a Catholic?

Once he is penetrated by her thought, the philosopher becomes aware that if there is to be an authentic encounter with her, much must be said of Edith Stein's spirituality to complete and complement what he perceives to be the ardor with which she pursued ideas. Yet he hesitates, for doubtless he would then enter a region where her effort was clearly not in vain, but to the benefit of her ultimate vocation in the history of the world. Yet such a task is beyond a philosopher's competence – so much so that it eludes him even while it attracts him – and he, like us, can only envisage the beginning of her spiritual adventure, that is, the first steps of her conversion.

1. When Edith Stein Converted

The word 'conversion' covers a group of phenomena which are anything but identical with one another. The most famous conversions are associated with what appears to be an upheaval which is both abrupt and irresistible. Just so, there is in sport too a *'conversion'* – that of the skier for example – who changes direction after stopping on landing, pivoting on the spot and taking off in another direction. Edith Stein's pace is rather that of slow motion, specified by what it keeps rather than by what it annuls. Edith Stein's conversion is one in which we find freely and respectively engaged a Jew, but also precisely a Woman, and finally a Philosopher. Without pretending to exhaust the mystery hidden in these three types of transitions, an examination of and a reflection on each deserves some attention.

My participation at birthday parties and other family feasts was never curtailed; and it remained my responsibility to provide the necessary occasional poetry. For the most part, I was totally unaware of the extent to which I had withdrawn from my family and of the pain this caused. I lived only for my studies and the aspirations they had awakened in me. I perceived them as my duty and felt in no way guilty of any injustice.

This constant exertion of my powers gave me an exhilarating feeling of living a very full life, and I saw myself as a richly endowed and highly privileged creature. On one occasion, our old principal, wishing to refer a pupil to me for tutoring, asked me to call on him. Naturally, he got around to inquiring how I was doing. When I replied with an enthusiastic, "Oh, I'm doing very well!" his large, round and somewhat protruding eyes opened even wider than usual.

"Well, one seldom hears that!" was his surprised comment.

One experience I had soon thereafter stands out in remarkably sharp contrast to this general euphoria of mine. At that time I slept in the same room as my sister Erna, and continued to do so until her marriage. There was as yet no electricity in our house, and we were using gas lamps. The lamp in our room was equipped with a dimmer; we had a habit of leaving the burner at its lowest setting at night, so that we could quickly turn up the light at any time. One morning our sister Frieda opened the door to our room and screamed in terror. She immediately perceived a strong odor of gas. Both of us lay in our beds, deathly white and apparently in a heavy stupor. The flame had gone out, and the gas was escaping. Frieda opened the window at once, turned off the jet, and wakened us. I returned to consciousness out of a state of sweet, dreamless rest, and what flashed through my mind upon coming to and grasping the situation was the thought, *"What a shame! Why couldn't they leave me in this deep peace forever?"* I myself *was shocked to discover that I clung to life so little.*

Even in my conscious daily life, I recall a time when the sun seemed to disappear. It was probably the summer of 1912 when I read the controversial novel Helmut Harringa. *Depicting student life, it portrayed in frighteningly vivid color the deplorable conditions in the fraternities with their senseless drinking requirements and the consequent moral aberrations. I was filled with such aversion that it took weeks before I recovered from it. I had lost all confidence in the persons with whom I associated daily; I went about as one unbearably burdened, and I was beyond finding enjoyment in anything at all. What cured me of this depression is highly significant. That year a great Bach Festival was given in Breslau. Bach was my favorite, so naturally I had a ticket for each of the performances: an organ concert, chamber music, and a gala evening of orchestral and vocal music. I no longer recall which oratorio was being presented that evening. I only know that Luther's defiant hymn, 'A Mighty Fortress' was included. I had always liked singing it in*

*our school devotions. When, in stirring
battle cry, the verse was sung*

And though this world with devils filled
Should threaten to undo us,
We will not fear,
. . . for truth will triumph through us.

*My pessimistic outlook vanished complete-
ly. True, the world might be evil; but if the
small group of friends in whom I had confidence and I strove with all our might, we
should certainly have done with all devils.*[1]

---

1   Edith Stein, *Life in a Jewish Family 1891–1916.*
     Translated by Josephine Koeppel, O.C.D. *The Collected
     Works of Edith Stein* (Washington: ICS Publications,
     1986), vol. 1, pp. 215–17.

2

The Conversion of a Jewess

Everyone knows that the world in which Edith Stein lived her early years was that of Judaism, a fairly hermetic world, but unwittingly it was the vehicle of what it represented figuratively in the perspective of the Unsuspected. A proof of this may be found in the memories she kept of those three feasts that lent their rhythm to the life of her family each year. There was first of all *Pesach*, then *Rosh Hashanah*, the new year, and finally *Yom Kippur*, the feast of reconciling expiation.

The first of these concerned the memory of a liberation whose reality it now celebrated: it is the feast of unleavened bread, the food with which the Hebrews had to content themselves during the flight from Egypt. Since Edith's father was dead from the time she was two years old, it was with her mother, brothers, and sisters that she took part in this holiday. The ritual had been adapted to the customs of central Europe, of course: one did not slaughter the lamb whose blood would mark the lintel of the doors to indicate those who were to be spared, but a special bread was distributed, the *Matzoh*, a term still used today. This bread was used throughout paschal week, all the more easily because it had been made without yeast. It was baked under the surveillance of the rabbinate attentive to this prescription, and in the task of removing every trace of yeast, families vied with one another in preparation for the feast in the care they took to rid the house of the least crumb of fermented bread. Even ordinary pans were forbidden for this reason, and those used the previous year were kept in the interval in the cellar or attic. All in all, it was a feast kept deliberately austere – seasoned with bitter herbs, and interrupted with prayers in memory of the vanquished deportation while texts from Exodus on the flight from Egypt were read.

Edith was the youngest one in the family and in the Pesach liturgy she took the role reserved for the youngest to pose a series of questions which gave the celebrant the occasion to explicate the rites.

Another feast, the feast of the New Year (Rosh Hashanah), perhaps less impressive, nonetheless remained sufficiently fresh in the memory of the young convert that she could describe its unfolding. Here too was a feast of newness but without alimentary restrictions: the bread distributed to the diners during two consecutive days was *challah*, a white woven bread, and for the occasion served in a round shape. On that night, for the feast began at the end of the day (which for the Jews is the beginning of the day), there were honey and raisins, nothing that was not succulent, for it is joyfully that one receives "the years of God."

The third feast to be considered seems more significant for Edith Stein's future: it is *Yom Kippur*, a summit of Jewish piety. It involves reconciliation, *Versöhnungstag*, and at the same time reparative expiations – *Sühne* is a German word associated with both ideas. Of course the ceremony had been simplified over time. One no longer followed the traditional rites; for example, the entry of the grandfather into the sanctuary of the Temple (its most secret part) to offer a sacrifice called significantly the sacrifice of expiation, after which one chased into the desert a goat bearing all the defects of the community. The Stein children who did not accompany their mother to the synagogue for the Jewish New Year – they were only brought at the end of the service – felt drawn, as indeed many non-Jewish lovers of music were, to the beauty of the chants proper to that vigil. A severe fast was part of the prescription of Yom Kippur, twenty-four hours without food or drink! To be certain that nothing would be wanting, one took the last meal before the feast day either before nightfall, despite the name employed, the *Nachtmahl*, a term borrowed perhaps from Catholic usage.[1]

From the way in which Edith Stein gives detailed accounts of the Jewish ceremonies that marked her childhood, it is clear that there is an authentic sympathy, along with the nostalgia of memories, putting at a certain remove her critical mind. No doubt as a philosopher, she considered this past with a sovereign eye, observing the lacks or deficiencies, but after her conversion had taken place, she came to judge the shadow by the reality of the light. And this, by means of a *presence*, at first unattended to but of which one day she would have a presentiment. Here is how.

It was at Frankfurt-on-Main. She had stopped in this city on the road which took her from Breslau, her native city, to Fribourg in Breisgau, the place of her studies, prompted to do so by a desire to make personally vivid the knowledge that she would have had of Frankfurt from the

1   In order to observe strictly the eucharistic fast, obligatory from midnight – and this no matter how long the distances to be traveled in the morning to the place of worship – parents would wake their children a little before midnight to feed them a last time before going: that was the Nachtmahl.

Gedanken und Erinnerungen of Goethe. Her friend, Pauline Reinach, of whom we shall hear more, served as her guide. The two entered the cathedral. And while they were there, silently contemplating the building, a simple woman, perhaps coming from her shopping in the square outside, her basket under arm, knelt for a short prayer as if for a visit. Edith Stein observed this, to her, unaccustomed sight. With unexpected simplicity, the woman acted like someone who had an appointment.

> *For me it was something completely new. In the synagogues and temples I knew, if one came it was for an office. Here, in the midst of daily affairs, someone came into an empty church as for a confidential exchange. I have never forgotten that.*

One is reminded in this connection of the peasant of Dombes who, whenever he had the occasion to pass the village church, stopped for a silent visit. His pastor – the curé d'Ars – who observed his unmoving lips, asked him what he could do in that way, apparently without murmuring a prayer. His answer was simply, "I look at him and he looks at me." In a letter of January 11, 1934, to an old school friend, another student of

Husserl, and like her a convert, Edith in her turn evoked the happiness one feels "in taking refuge in the silence of the choir to think over before the tabernacle whatever had happened." As for herself, whenever she experienced a philosophical difficulty, it was again "before the tabernacle" that she came to regain her courage (*der Mut aufrichten*) "when she felt depressed by the knowledge others had."

ON WOMAN

*Woman's nature is determined by her
original vocation of spouse and mother.
One depends on the other. The body of
woman is fashioned "to be one flesh" with
another and to nurse new human life in
itself. A well-disciplined body is an accom-
modating instrument for the mind which
animates it; at the same time, it is a source
of power and a habitat for the mind. Just
so, woman's soul is designed to be subordi-
nate to man in obedience and support; it is
also fashioned to be a shelter in which other
souls may unfold. Spiritual companionship
and spiritual motherliness are not limited
to the physical spouse and mother relation-
ships, but they extend to all people with
whom a woman comes into contact.*

The soul of woman must therefore be
expansive *and open to all human beings;*
it *must* be quiet *so that no small weak
flame will be extinguished by stormy
winds;* warm *so as not to benumb fragile
buds;* clear, *so that no vermin will settle in
dark corners and recesses;* self-contained,

so that no invasions from without can imperil the inner life; empty of itself, *in order that extraneous life may have room in it; finally,* mistress of itself *and also of the body, so that the entire person is readily at the disposal of all.*

That is an ideal image of the feminine soul. The soul of the first woman was formed for this purpose, and so, too, was the soul of the Mother of God. In all other women since the Fall, there is an embryo of such development, but it needs particular cultivation if it is not to be suffocated among rank weeds shooting up around it.

Woman's soul should be expansive; *nothing human should be alien to it. Evidently, it has a natural predisposition to such an end: on average, its principal interest is directed to people and human relations. But, if one leaves the natural instinct to itself, this is expressed in a manner apart from its objective. Often the interest is chiefly mere curiosity, mere desire to get to know people and their circumstances; sometimes it is a real avidity to penetrate alien areas. If this instinct is simply indulged in, then nothing is won either for the soul itself or for other souls.*

It goes out of itself, so to speak, and remains standing outside of itself. It loses itself, without giving anything to others. This is unfruitful, indeed, even detrimental. Woman's soul will profit only if it goes abroad to search *and to bring home the hidden* treasure *which rests in every human soul, and which can enrich not only her soul but also others; and it will profit only if it searches and bears home the well-known or hidden* burden *which is laid on every human soul. Only the one who stands with wholesome awe before human souls will search in such a manner, one who knows that human souls are the kingdom of God, who knows that one may approach them only if one is* sent *to them. But whoever is sent will find that which she is seeking, and whoever is so sought will be found and saved. Then the soul does not remain standing on the outside but, on the contrary, carries its booty home; and its expanses* must *widen in order to be able to take in what it carries.*

The soul has to be quiet, *for the life which it must protect is timid and speaks only faintly; if the soul itself is in tumult, it will not hear this life which will soon be completely silenced and will disappear from the soul. I wonder whether one can say that the feminine soul is fashioned by nature for this? At first sight, the contrary seems to be true. Women's souls are in commotion so much and so strongly: commotion itself makes much noise; and in addition the soul is urged to express its agitation. Nevertheless, the faculty for this quiet must be there; otherwise it could not be so profoundly practiced as it is, after all, by many women: those women in whom one takes refuge in order to find peace, and who have ears for the softest and most imperceptible little voices.*[1]

1. *The Collected Works of Edith Stein*, translated by Freda Mary Oben, (Washington: ICI Publications, 1987), vol. 2 (*Woman*), pp. 118–20.

3

THE CONVERSION OF A WOMAN

One must also speak of the conversion of a feminist. We have just seen the role the simple example of an ordinary uncultivated woman played in the evolution of this intellectual. Her silent adoration attested to a presence, which explained the visit to a place Edith would later learn was not only architecturally impressive, it was inhabited. To say now that hers was the conversion of a woman may seem a banal truism, even out of place. For those who come to Christ "there is neither man nor woman . . ." Yet each one comes with all that he is, and by means of that inalienable capital, which is not so much a burden as a responsibility offered, an obligation held.

Edith Stein was the product of a feminine milieu as much as of traditions of a Jewish stamp. Without any doubt, along with her mother one can count her mother's brothers and many sisters, fifteen in all, their names committed to memory as "in religion classes one memorized the twelve sons of Jacob." This produced a rhythmic litany: Bianca, Cilla, Jakob, Gustel, Selma, Siege, Berthold, Mälchen, David, Mika, Eugen, Emil,

Alfred, Clara, Emma. Edith Stein's mother is fourth on the list, Gustel – the diminutive of Auguste, a feminine name in German. She would be left alone after the sudden death of her husband, not only alone in the home but alone at the head of the business – dealing in wood – with seven mouths to feed (four of the eleven children were dead at any early age). Only a little younger than Erna, Edith was the youngest. She was therefore raised by women.

Does it follow from that that she was more attentive to caring for her person? The simple fact that in this regard she later recognized a defect in herself attests to the presence of this aspect of femininity. Living in the country, things of fashion had less importance than learning how to bind sheaves (with no other means than straw), or to watch the cows. Dress was not therefore the first of her concerns and perhaps she kept from this period a free and somewhat wild appearance. On the other hand, later, notably at Speyer where she taught in a college run by the Dominicans, she was more careful in dress, seeing how attentive the young women were, who were doubtless mischievous and ready to judge by appearances. This same concern for her appearance is shown when she began to give conferences throughout Germany, beginning with Günterstal, where she boarded with the Oblates of St. Benedict, some kilometers from Fribourg: she was concerned enough about it to consult one of her old comrades, also a student of Husserl's, as to which dress she should wear.[1]

More characteristic and more original than the others, Edith Stein very soon became involved in politics because of the "feminine question," which, she tells us, was a hot topic among social democrats. This is all the more noteworthy because she was teased about it by her colleagues. Thus on the holiday at the end of the year, when the professors composed predictions for their stu-

---

1   Miss Jägerschmitt, the last survivor of the students of Edmund Husserl, was also a convert to Catholicism, but coming from Protestantism. Later she entered the Benedictine Oblates of Saint Lioba at Günterstal. She became a nurse during the war and at the express command of her superior would accompany Husserl and his wife when he was hospitalized in Rapallo. It is to this precious witness over a long period that we dedicated our book *Edith Stein, Philosopher* on the sixtieth anniversary of her religious profession. A film by Heidi Hölzer was devoted to her on German television, with a scene in which the book was presented to her. She was over a hundred when she died in 1996. It was in her company that we went for the first time to Husserl's tomb in the little cemetery in Günterstal where he is at rest.

dents in rhyming lines, this was the quatrain dedicated to her:

> The equality of man and woman
> Is what this Suffragette demands
> And so for sure one day we'll see
> Her head of that new Ministry.

And so, with a provocative air, sure of herself, bold because sufficiently conscious of her value, the young militant on behalf of the equality of rights for men and women will later ask for its application to the world of the university. She would be the first, having become doctor of philosophy – and the one who registered her title could have added "Miss" – to ask officially that women be admitted as well to present a *habilitation* thesis for the professorate. Toward the end of her life, looking back at these struggles of a former time , she would survey the road that had led finally to a successful liberation.

> *Nowadays young women get their baccalaureate and are inscribed on the university rolls without knowing the meetings, resolutions, petitions addressed to the Reichstag and to the governments of states that brought it about that in 1901 the*

> *doors of the German university were*
> *opened to women.*

She was accordingly a dedicated woman, conscious of her obligation to femininity, who unwittingly approached an encounter that changed her direction completely. Interestingly enough, the road that took her there was prepared by other women, both Catholic and Protestant. Mention has already been made of Pauline Reinach, who married Husserl's principal assistant at Göttingen, a philosopher whose research had centered more and more on the phenomenon of religion. Called up into the army, he took the occasion of a Christmas leave to be baptized, himself a Jew, along with his wife. Edith Stein knew nothing of this at the time it happened; she only knew that a comrade called to military service had come back from the front to take a training course to qualify as chief of an artillery battery. Nonetheless, Edith was struck by the change in him during this leave. "He claimed to have discovered at the front that he was not equipped for philosophy. From now on he would occupy himself with religious questions."[2] Shortly afterward, news came of his death

2   Letter of Edith Stein to F. Kaufman, January 12,
      1917. Later she would find another philosopher to be
      'changed,' namely Heidegger, when she visited him

on the field of honor – a hero's death, in the accepted expression. The young widow, faced with the task of arranging his papers, appealed to their common friend to help in a task where she felt philosophically inadequate. Edith agreed and came, expecting to find the new widow plunged into grief. To her great surprise what she found in the home of her friend was "Christian hope." The impression this made was far greater than that of Max Scheler, the hitherto unknown Catholic who was making such an impression among those teaching at Göttingen.

It was by intermediary of another Protestant woman friend that she made the decisive acquaintance with an enormously impressive personage emerging unexpectedly from a past age, Teresa of Avila. We are in August 1921: Edith Stein is staying in the home of the Conrad-Martiuses, at Bergzabern in the Palitinate where they cultivated fruits and vegetables. On an occasion when Hedwig had to be absent, she showed Edith the library. It was all hers to peruse at her leisure. And then the unexpected encounter.

> in April, 1930, but changed in a far different sense: "very different from before, full of projects," concerning university politics and its alignment with the aims of the regime, in fact, already put in orbit, and which he would enact as Rector of faculties.

I took at random a large book with the title
The Life of Saint Teresa of Jesus, written by herself. *I began to read and I was
immediately caught up in it and could not
stop until I reached the end. When I closed
the book, I said to myself: There is the
truth.*

Thus in the early hours of the morning after a
night passed in the company of a Spanish religious, the destiny of Edith Stein appeared sealed.
It was Teresa's name she wished to take at the baptism she decided on then and there, but which
would only take place on the first of the following
January. She would add, by way of gratitude, the
name of the friend at whose home and because of
whom the meeting had occurred: Hedwig.

In the interval, she acquired a Catholic cate-
chism in order to initiate herself into the teach-
ings of the Church. She bought a Benedictine
Missal (Schott) of a kind then commonly used in
Germany. Thus instructed, she dared to attend
Mass, where nothing came as a surprise:
"Nothing was strange to me, thanks to my studies
I understood the most minuscule element of the
ceremony." A woman of thought, she acquired
knowledge.

That done, she decided to follow the priest to

the presbytery after his thanksgiving and without fanfare asked him for baptism. We are at Bergzabern in the Palatinate: Zabern is where the Conrad-Martiuses had their farm. The pastor, a bit nonplused, replied that baptism requires preparation. He got an answer in the vocabulary familiar in the university: *Prüfen Sie mich! Test me!* The *truth* which she had discovered after a night of reading was thus linked to a teaching: proof, if needed, that hers was a conversion of a woman with a heart but also that of a woman with a head.

But before examining the professional slant of this last aspect, let us emphasize a point about her femininity which her biographers have tended to simplify. According to some, she repudiated at the outset all thought of marriage. This is true from the time of her baptism, since she will later tell us that from that day she had wished immediately to enter the Carmel of her dear St. Teresa. But to place a decision for celibacy earlier, is to move a little too swiftly.[3]

For one willing to read between the lines, there is a long conversation suggesting otherwise that Edith had with Hans Lipp, her fellow student at Göttingen, which she reports in detail. She and Hans Lipp shared a long train journey together,

3   See Hilda Graef, *Edith Stein, The Scholar and the Cross.*

one taking him back to the front after a leave, and her to her studies at Fribourg. Were it not for the constraints imposed by the war on their different plans, it seems clear that he would then have been her heart's choice, and she his. The most able of Edith Stein's biographers has recognized this, "If Hans had made a proposal of marriage to her then, as was the good and proper form of procedure, she would have become his fiancée, but God, it seems, had other plans for her."[4] For him as well as her. The day when Hans, discharged, came to visit her at the Carmel of Cologne, Edith could only confirm her engagement. "Now, she told him, it is too late, for from now on Another had placed his hand on me forever."[5]

This did not prevent her from remaining faithful to the memory of Hans Lipp, to the point of making particular mention of him when she learned of his death on the Russian Front in the first years of the Second World War.[6] In this regard, as on other occasions, there applies, for him as well as for her, a reflection which guides

4   R. Leuven, ESW, tome X, p. 27.

5   A document preserved at the Carmel of Cologne, cited by Leuven, p. 27.

6   See Florent Gaboriau, *Edith Stein Philosophe* (Paris: FAC, 1988), p. 75.

the abandonment of our destinies to God: "What was not found in my plan, God had put into his."[7]

It was in God's plan that this woman, who was not only conscious of her femininity at the moment when she felt herself called to conversion, but as a woman philosopher was also concerned with the Truth to be discovered. That indeed was her own conclusion in those early morning hours after finishing reading the autobiography of Saint Teresa. "There is the truth."

7   ESW, t. II, p. 110.

ON DEATH
(With Reference to Heidegger)

Death is the end of bodily life and of every-
thing connected with it. Even more, it is a
somber portal: it has to be gone through,
but what then? That "What then?" is the
real question concerning death. Is there an
answer to the question before we go
through the door?

Men who have looked death in the face
and then returned to life are the exception.
The majority of men are confronted with
death by the death of another. Heidegger
affirms that we cannot "live" the experi-
ence of another's death; we certainly do not
"live" it in the same way as our own death.
Still, the agony and death of another are
fundamental realities, essential for our
comprehension of our own being and of
being human in general. If we did not con-
stantly see other men die, we would not
believe in the end of our own existence; we
would not comprehend the agony that it
inspires in us, and many people would

never face it in its nudity (that is, without being clothed with the fear of this or that).

In childhood, death is generally represented as "being no longer in the world." There were certain beings who were in our entourage, near or far, who disappear, and we are told that they are dead. So long as we do not know anything more, we feel no fear, no fright, before death. At that moment there is manifested what Heidegger calls the "Man stirbt" (one dies), which consists in knowing that all men, one day or another, leave the world in which we live and that that day will come for us as well. This is a fact that we do not doubt. Yet we have no experience that makes us truly "realize" this fact; it is not an event that we would wait for. Also it leaves us cold, without uneasiness. For the child, this unconcern is natural and healthy. But to persist in this attitude into the age of an adult, perhaps throughout life, is not truly to live one's life. In order for a life to be fully human and for existence to be truly understood, we must have our eyes open to the last things. A child aware of the nature of things will become uneasy at the disappearance of persons he has known; he wants to know what it means to be dead. The explanations given him cause him to reflect on death and suffice to shake the unawareness involved in "One dies." But what will certainly shake it is the sight of a dead person. The duty to take part in a burial can already have this effect on a sensitive child. When the coffin becomes visible as the flowers are removed, when it is placed in the tomb, then the feelings of fright will come concerning one's own inevitable disappearance, and there will be perhaps a feeling of revulsion at the sight of the inanimate body.

If no religious education, with its teaching on eternal life, has given another sense to death, the sight of the dead enforces that representation of "being no longer in the world," and above all of disanimation – in the conception of the subject while alive, vitality predominates over the things of the spirit. Heidegger must come to an impasse on this consideration, for it forces him to take seriously the problem of body and soul in their reciprocal relationship, which he has excluded apriori. In all times, the experience of death has imposed on the artless

man the question of the soul's destiny
under this form.

It is even more necessarily imposed as
long as one does not simply see someone
dead but assists at a death. Whoever has
witnessed this agony can no longer remain
at the level of banality of "One dies." One
is present at the violent rupture of a natural unity. And when the struggle is over,
the man who has engaged in it, or for
whom it has run its course, is no longer
there. What remains of him is no longer
himself. Where is the one who made him a
living being? If we find no answer to that
question, the sense of death escapes us.

Faith has an answer.[1]

1   ESW, VI, "Martin Heideggers Existential-philoso-
phie," pp. 104–6.

4

THE CONVERSION OF A PHILOSOPHER

Her condition as a Jewess and as a woman gives place to a choice on the level of her profession – and in this case *Beruf* (*call*) leads to *Berufung* (*calling*) – it would not be alien to her "vocation." The matter is not evident apriori, quite the opposite, if one thinks of the case of Husserl's chief assistant, Reinach, who seemed to detach himself from philosophy the moment his eyes were opened to the gate of a new world.[1] Does the spiritual universe leave any place for the rational universe? The answer is certainly Yes in the case of Edith Stein. When she in her turn converted it was not to renounce her profession but on the contrary to deepen it.

A woman with a mind, and all the more so in the choice that led her where she did not think to go, Edith Stein had already had the occasion to express her determination on this point. In discussions with friends at Breslau, including her

1 See Florent Gaboriau, *Edith Stein Philosophe*, *op. cit.*, p. 48. The philosopher's wife, Pauline Reinach, would also convert later and enter the religious life, with the Benedictines of Ermeton in Belgium.

sister Erna, who had chosen to study medicine, she had taken a position on the question whether one could manage both marriage and a profession:

> *I myself, she said, have always been certain that I would not sacrifice my profession for any price.*[2]

The same was true later when her encounter with Jesus took place: it was not only a child of Jewish origin who turned toward him, it was not only a woman conscious of her identity as "feminist and radical,"[3] it was a professional philosopher, mature in the exercise of the demands of reflection, who then took on a new vigor of thought. This would have borne, or would bear, one thinks, on the femininity itself, its riches and its limits.

> *Woman tends to the living and personal: she has a great desire for the absolute. To cherish, guard and protect are her natural, true and maternal desires.*[4]

And as for a less laudable characteristic:

2   ESW, VII, p. 96.
3   Text of 1931, cited by Hilda Graef, *op. cit.*, p. 93.
4   *Ibid.*, p. 94

> *A woman is inclined to be interested in her*
> *own person and to expect from others the*
> *same interest.*[5]

But rather than remain on a level of generality
with regard to the respective aptitudes of men and
women, where much of the mystery of identities
slips away, Edith Stein's reflection bears thence-
forth on what she can observe of the life of reli-
gions.

It is certain that for a long time the matter left
her indifferent. Submerged in work, busy with
deciphering Husserl's stenographic manuscripts,
she had no interest in what is called "praying" –
unless by way of badinage on the matter: "Pray
for me or rather for the *Ideas*."[6] Yet the death of
Adolph Reinach effected an opening for her when
she would discover, in the course of classifying his
papers, some "Notes on the philosophy of religion" which astonished her. Some of the pages
seemed to her "so beautiful" that she made the
suggestion: shouldn't these be published in the
Jahrbuch, at least under the title of fragments?
With respect to her own work she mentions

5   *Ibid.*, p. 96.
6   The title of the book on which she was working. This
    notion of prayer is formulated in a letter to Roman
    Ingarden. (ESW, VIII, p. 21)

something hitherto absent: "I have left open the possibility of a philosophy of religion."[7] A gesture of acceptance, one might think, to the colleague prematurely gone, cut down by destiny, whose sacrifice, recently *Christianized*, worked to the benefit of the friend occupied with classifying his *Nachlass* and brought about this opening.

Still one cannot say that Edith Stein had awaited this development of thought, in its way professionally induced, to raise the question of God, which had been present in her circle from childhood.[8] To the degree that Edith was surrounded by an abundance of observances, she was intrigued, but she was never for example preoccupied to know what the ringing of the Angelus bells in all the Catholic churches meant. There was a young Jewish comrade, however, whose attitude seemed to her to be one of excessive zeal and ostentation, whom one day she asked for his idea of God. His reply: *Geist! Spirit!* – which, especially in German, is deceptive because of its very vagueness. That is, "a stone rather than bread,"[9] and apriori indigestible by one with a real

7   ESW, VIII, p. 40.

8   That is why, it seems to me, that, using terms strictly, it is too much to say that she had been an atheist during her youth – indifferent would capture it better.

9   ESW, VII, p. 182.

hunger. The impression she came away with was like that created by a rabbi's discourse at a funeral service.

> *I had heard, she wrote, many such discourses. A retrospective look was cast over the life of the deceased, the good that he had done was mentioned, and the grief of his relatives noted. There was really nothing truly consoling. Of course, it was said, raising the voice: When the body dissolves into dust, the Spirit returns to God who gave it. But the words did not seem to contain any faith in a personal life, no belief in a reunion after death.* [10]

This goes far beyond the level of a critical observation as does her remark about her family when she notes that her brothers to whom fell the task of saying the prayers in the place of their dead father, did so with little dignity, not to say offhandedly. The youngest brother notably, when called on in the absence of the older, did not conceal the fact that he was inwardly amused by it all. [11] So too for the New Year, although her

10 *Ibid.*, p. 56.
11 *Ibid.*, p. 44.

mother went to the synagogue, the children took the day off. "Free from school, on that day we had the time to devote to reading and we equipped ourselves accordingly."[12] Nor did our philosopher dwell on the strict formalism, save to point out its vanity, as when a comrade quite blithely confided his prudent rule: "When I don't know how to define it, I consider it forbidden," and for that reason refused a snack she offered him on the ground that it was not kosher. Another example of the maximalism that put her off: one day she was walking with this same comrade who suddenly remembered an errand he had to run at a place nearby and, to move faster, took his briefcase in both hands. As soon as he did so, he remembered the day was the Sabbath when one may not carry anything. When he came back, he excused himself with this self-justification: "I did nothing wrong, since it is in the street that one ought not to carry anything; inside, it is permitted." And, after all, they were in the lobby! Here is Edith's commentary; "That was one of the Talmudic subtleties that repelled me, but I kept silent."[13] Could one then say that Edith Stein had been until the age of twenty-one an atheist? Her biographers all

12   *Ibid.*, VII, p. 45
13   *Ibid.*, p. 181–82.

suggest this – unless there is an exception I do not know of – even in the excellent film devoted to her.[14] The source of this seems to have been badly interpreted. It is a question of a letter from Professor B. Rosenmöller, dated March 24, 1946, the original of which can be found in the Carmel of Cologne. But the letter does not give much precise information about Edith Stein's youth. Indeed, if one is to use words exactly, it is the adjective "indifferent" that applies to her at this age rather than "atheist." As happens with many young people, and by her own observation, Edith was very bored by the services of the Synagogue where her mother took her with her sisters. But it is to go well beyond any evidence to draw from this a fixed attitude that could be called in any strict sense atheism. The lack of a religious appetite extended into her student days, when she was interested in other things, to the point that, later, she thought back on this time in order to locate in that desert the indicators that enabled her to escape from it. The important thing for her, it seems, lay in the sense that was or was not given to death, which was present all around her. Out of despair, first one uncle, then another, had committed suicide. She loved them both very

14 *Die Jüdin* of Marta Meszaros, Katholisches Filmwerk, 1995.

much and withheld judgment on what they had done, but it seemed to her a species of desertion "from which the genuine believer is held back, of course, by his submission to the will of God."[15]

So it was that the reflective conversion that was preparing itself within her did not dispense with the need for rational estimates, as in the way that the Christian attitude toward death played an essential role in her appreciation of that critical event. We have already noted her disappointment in the rabbinic funeral discourse; it contrasted dramatically with what she was offered at the burial of a Catholic scholar.

> *When much later I attended a Catholic funeral for the first time, the difference made a deep impression on me. Although he had been a well-known scientist, there was no question of his merits and one did not even mention the name he had made famous. It was by his baptismal name that the poor soul was recommended to the mercy of God. Yet what powerful consolation and peace there was in the words of the Liturgy which accompanied the deceased to his eternity.[16]*

15   ESW, VII, p. 56.

16   *Ibid.*, p. 57

Already discoverable in the course of the Old Testament, faith in the resurrection is explicit at the heart of the New Testament. From now on there is no doubt: "Happy the dead who fall asleep in the Lord!" (Ap 14: 13). Such a faith is inseparable from that bearing on "the Just Judge" (2 Tim 4: 8). It is a faith that defines the salvation for which humans are called to strive and which, the test having been passed, makes "them at rest from their pains, for their works accompany them." (Ap 14: 13) A faith whose statute is an introduction to the definitive, although provisory with respect to the body, yet marked at its last moment for what it is to come: an unheard-of perspective where one will be, as Saint Thomas says, not only free of evil but a participant in the glory of God, associated with him to the point of identity, according to the promise of Jesus and thanks to his merits: "That they may be one in us, as we are one." (Jn 22: 22)[17]

---

17 "Non solum salvi erimus a malis (a peccato et a poena), sed etiam gloriamur in Deo. . . . Per hoc quod erimus idem in futuro cum Ipso, Jn 22, 22: 'Ut sint unum in nobis sicut et nos unum sumus.'" St. Thomas Aquinas, *Commentary on the Epistle to the Romans* (Marietti, n. 405).

On Spiritual Discernment

1. Should discretio – *discernment – be considered a Gift of the Holy Spirit?*

It cannot be considered either as one of the seven gifts or as an eighth. The gift of discernment is found in each of the gifts; one might even say that the seven gifts are diverse expressions of this unique gift.

The gift of fear discerns in God the divina majestas *and measures the infinite distance between the holiness of God and our baseness.*

The gift of piety recognizes in God pietas, *the fatherly goodness toward which man turns with the look of an infant, respectfully loving, capable of distinguishing what is due the Father who is in heaven.*

Counsel (prudence) seems more clearly to be a gift of discernment: the discernment of that which it is fitting to do in each situation.

One is inclined to think that the gift of fortitude is something purely voluntary. But the separation between prudence which recognizes the path to be taken, and a fortitude that imposes itself blindly, makes sense only in the natural order. Where the Holy Spirit reigns, man's spirit lets itself be guided without resistance. Prudence determines without reticence practical behavior, fortitude receives the light of prudence. Together, these gifts allow a man to adapt himself to the circumstances of life.

Submitted without resistance to the Spirit, man is ready to face whatever comes to him. This light, insofar as it is the gift of knowledge, permits him to see clearly everything created and every event in its ordination to the Eternal, to comprehend it in its structure and to recognize its proper place and true weight.

As understanding, this light introduces him to the depths of the Divinity and makes manifest to him in all its clarity revealed Truth.

And in its fulfillment in the gift of wisdom, it unites him to the Holy Trinity and gives him access to the eternal Source, to all that proceeds from it and which is held within it, according to that movement of the divine Life in which Knowledge and Love are fully united.

2. Discretio *as an intellectual act.*

Holy discernment is radically distinguished from human intelligence, even the most acute.

This act of thought does not discern by a process which advances step by step, as the human mind does; it does not discern by analysis and synthesis, by comparing and collecting, by conclusion or by proof. Like the eye in the clearness of day, discernment sees without effort the clear contour of things. Penetration into details does not impede the complete view of internal connections. The higher the climber goes, the wider the scope of his vision, until he arrives at the summit and takes in the whole horizon. Thus, illumined by the eternal light, the eye of the spirit embraces the far-off, nothing confused remains, nothing remains indiscernible. With unity plenitude increases, to the point that, in the undivided rays of divine light the entire world becomes visible: magna visio. [1]

1   Waltraud Herbstrith, *Edith Stein – Ways to Inner Peace* (Aschaffenburg, Germany: Kaffke, 1987), pp. 96–97.

5

CONVERSION EXTENDED OVER TIME

Nevertheless conversion is only a first step in the direction of what will follow. Already, there is neither Greek nor Jew, neither man nor woman, neither philosopher nor rustic: there is, defying all our distinctions, the wisdom of the Messiah, Christ, who provokes ascension. And in Edith Stein's case that would be the ascent of Carmel, the ascent of Calvary.

What presented itself to be converted in the case of Edith Stein was assuredly her Judaism, her femininity, her philosophy. And by way of corollary one can comprehend, in the interior of her essential conversion, a manner of intellectual conversion to the thought of the Common Doctor of whom before-hand she had had no idea but who from then on inspired her. She explains this last point with a smile.

> *Saint Thomas was no longer content with only a few hours set aside for his benefit, he wanted me entirely. . . . I surrendered myself at Breslau in order to advance in all calmness in the great work that I had undertaken.*

That is what she wrote from Beuron on March 28, 1931, to a teaching colleague, Sister Callista Kopf, O.P., making allusion to the little bit of time that she could devote to work, given the responsibilities that were hers at Speyer in the course of the year. It was no longer just a question of her German translation of the *De veritate* (*Disputed Question on Truth*), but of an essay in ontology entitled *Act and Potency*, which would occupy her throughout the summer of 1931: a first go at what would become, revised at Münster and then at the Carmel of Cologne, her posthumous work, *Finite and Eternal Being*.

She remained therefore more and more faithful to her vocation as philosopher, just as she remained faithful to her Judaism and to her femininity, but in a new manner. The conference she gave January 31, 1931, at Ludwigshafen under the title "The Mystery of Christmas,"[1] made the link between the birth of Jesus under the old alliance and his death on the cross which sealed the new, not to abolish the first but to fulfill it. Likewise, "the truth to which phenomenology introduced her was to expand under her own spiritual predispositions."[2] From this point of view, it is strange

1   *Das Weihnachtsmysterium.*

2   Philibert Secretan, preface to *La prière de l'Eglise* (Geneva: Ad Solem, 1995), p. 9.

that one should discuss the philosophy of Edith Stein, making appeal only to the initial period (Scheler, Husserl), while passing over in silence the thinker with whom, at the end, she was fulfilled, even to the conversion of intellect, namely, Thomas Aquinas.[3]

It is to this last, indeed, that she referred her old comrade from Göttingen, Hedwig Conrad-Martius, as to a source newly discovered, in speaking to her of the attempt that seemed to her fruitful, "to go from Scholasticism to phenomenology, and vice versa."[4] This suggestion would be reflected in the work of this correspondent who published an important review article on it.[5] In addition, Edith Stein offered to this same philosopher a chance to cast a critical eye on the work which was then in preparation.

3   Not to forget the presence and influence, sometimes decisive, of another great medieval thinker, Duns Scotus.

4   Letter of November 24, 1933. Incomprehensively, this letter is absent from ESW, VIII, where it should have its place. Happily, it can be found in Edith Stein, *Briefe an Hedwig Conrad-Martius* (Munich: Kösel, 1960), p. 15.

5   "Natur und Gnade, nach hl. Thomas von Aquin: Untersuchungen über die Wahrheit [Nature and Grace according to St. Thomas Aquinas: Inquiries into Truth]" in *Catholica* (April, 1934).

Yes, if you would care to undertake to show your god-daughter the existential significration of the obligation you took on, I will send you this monstrous opus, but of course in order that you might give it a rigorous criticism, a radical critique, for I have often asked myself if, in philosophical work in general, I do not go beyond my own capacities.[6]

A modesty in no way feigned, since one finds her having recourse at another time to the judgment of a colleague, presumed to be more informed. She was not unaware of the handicap involved in coming to the great medieval master late. She could write with authority and without any hesitation a long appendix on the philosophy of Heidegger,[7] while feeling the need to submit the rest of the manuscript to the judgment of a leading figure on the Middle Ages.

I always have the feeling, in these domains, of being a complete dilettante, and that is

6   Letter of November 24, 1933, *op. cit.*, p. 17.

7   Not that this effort did not require much work: "For several weeks, I have been torturing myself with an appendix on the existential philosophy of Heidegger."(ESW, IX, p. 64).

why I hope to have the judgment of a specialist.[8]

That said, she wanted to be a hundred leagues from indiscreet proselytism, as is evident in the kind of relation she established with the Husserls after her conversion. It no longer was a question merely of thought, it also involved an existential adherence. They themselves had taken the step to Christianity when they were baptized in Vienna, in the Lutheran Church, when the philosopher was twenty-seven years old, and their three children had been raised in the Protestant religion. While assistant to the master she revered, Edith Stein had retained her freedom of thought and that led her to resign the post to which Martin Heidegger succeeded shortly afterward. When, after having "turned in her portfolio,"[9] she found her old master again after eight years of separation, a step had been taken: in the meantime she had become a Catholic. Hence the inevitable exchange bearing on this new orientation. But notice the reserve, without sacrificing frankness, that Edith had to observe.

8   Letter of August 20, 1936, *Edith Stein's Briefe* (Munich: Kösel, p. 42).

9   The phrase is hers: letter to Roman Ingarden, July 6, 1917. (ESW, VIII, p. 28.)

*I spoke to him in all frankness. His wife
seemed hostile to my conversion, but to each
of her expressions of incomprehension, he
himself replied in terms so beautiful and
profound that I had almost nothing to add.
Nonetheless it is important, I think, to
guard oneself against illusion here. It is
certainly well to touch on these problems,
but then the responsibility of the interlocutor is increased, as is mine. I have no doubt
that prayer and sacrifice are of far greater
weight than anything we might say. . . .
After each encounter, when the discussion
turned into powerlessness, the pressing
necessity of a personal holocaust was
imposed on me.*[10]

A phrase like that just read appears premonitory
in the light of what followed. After it, she
returned to the modesty of the day-to-day.

10 A letter dated Septuagesima 1930 to Sister
Adelgundis, a friend of the Husserl family. Very reticent at this time with respect to Catholicism, as
Madame Heidegger would be throughout her life,
Malville Husserl would at the end join Edith Stein,
herself converting to Catholicism after the war. In the
meantime, she had taken refuge in Belgian religious
houses, which enabled her, not without risk, to escape
deportation.

Whether our present form of life is more or less good, we can at bottom know nothing. What we are sure of is that we are here below to work out our salvation and that of the souls that are linked to ours.

Conversion is a movement inversely parallel to that which seeks diversion or even deviation. The renegade inscribes his distancing from God in the calculations of his life. For it can be advantageous, in the eyes of the world and with an eye to one's career, to follow a different path than that taken by Edith Stein. There is a flagrant contrast in this respect with the evolution of Martin Heidegger at this same time. In a letter to a priest friend who had blessed his marriage fourteen months earlier, the new assistant of Husserl announced the decision he had taken to repudiate from then on what he called "the Catholic system."

Some years later, the recipient of that letter himself, an old comrade of Heidegger's in the seminary of Fribourg, in his private journal compared the itineraries which, going in contrary directions, crossed one another.

How destinies diverge! Edith Stein attained a great reputation in the philo-

sophical domain early on, and then she made herself small and humble, a Catholic finally, and has retired to the Dominican convent at Speyer to devote herself to the work of silence. Heidegger, beginning under the colors of Catholic philosophy, became an unbeliever, distanced himself from the Church, and achieved celebrity and is seen surrounded by the corporation of philosophers who make up his circle.[11]

The circle around Edith Stein could only contract, the more so that, confronted from now on with the Common Doctor, she had a feeling of her smallness.

> *This recognition of my own limits has increased rapidly in me in the course of these last months.*[12]

She had doubts about herself philosophically, whereas in the past she had been reproached

11 The "Journal of Krebs," cited by Hugo Ott, *Martin Heidegger: A Political Life*, translated by Allan Blunden (New York: Basic Books, 1993), p. 112.

12 ESW, VIII, p. 122. A letter to Hedwig Conrad-Martius, November 13, 1932.

rather for an excess of self-confidence.[13] Quite apropos, Father Krebs, cited earlier, recalled at the end of his reflections a remark of Jesus: "I bless you, Father, because you have hidden these things from the great and powerful and revealed them to the lowly." He himself was then dean of the Faculty of Theology at Fribourg but had to abandon teaching three years later when Heidegger was Rector. And it is true that in the eyes of the world Edith Stein would today be better treated – with respect to her thought – if, when the storm had passed, she had reappeared after the war like Hannah Arendt, onetime mistress of Heidegger, to provide us with her interesting reflections on that strange period when highway bandits held power, to the applause of the bamboozled crowd and their guides, the "philosophers," of course.

It is well known that Heidegger seems never to have felt, or in any case expressed, any remorse for a period of his life when his convictions came to be diametrically opposed to those of Edith Stein. Instead, his family had the idea, in order to rehabilitate him, of suggesting that there had been an intervention on his part on behalf of the

13 This alludes to a remark made to her by her friend Hedwig Conrad: *ein allzu naives Selbstvertraen*. Letter of November 13, 1932. ESW, VIII, p. 122.

Carmelite, and that she made a special trip from Cologne to Fribourg to seek the favor of special protection.

This legend was publicly launched by means of a Japanese student of Heidegger's[14] who had a perhaps excusable ignorance of the rigors of the Carmelite cloister. Did it have the retrospective effect of whitewashing the guilty party? Even Hugo Ott, a historian without guile, had no knowledge of this maneuver, and I myself was unaware of it when I published *Edith Stein, Philosopher.* I became aware of it by means of a letter discovered in the course of visits to Messkirch, the native village of Heidegger, thanks to the help of one of his compatriots. I have a photocopy of this letter, which is addressed to Hermann Heidegger, the philosopher's oldest son, on July 29, 1978, by Sister Maria-Amata Neyer of the Carmel of Cologne, which firmly denied the existence of any such event, already unlikely for anyone who knew the strict rule of the monastic cloister.[15]

---

14 Paul Shih-Yi Hsiao, in *Errinerung an Martin Heidegger* (Pfufflingen, Germany:_Günther Neske, 1977), p. 122 ff. Manipulated by his informants, he imagined letters and telegrams from the Carmelite imploring the philosopher's help.

15 I verified the authenticity of this letter with Sister

Withdrawn from the world by the Word of God,[16] it is clear that Edith Stein never had any idea of such a plea. The only personal allusion to Heidegger that one finds in the letters of the Carmelite was occasioned by the death of Husserl, a disturbing one: "*Und Heidegger?*" She asked, wondering what his attitude toward the event was.[17]

There is another remark of Edith Stein that seems to me premonitory, or in any case worthy of meditation: *Prüfen Sie mich! Test me!* What she asked in these words of the pastor of Bergzabern, when he understandably was reticent to baptize her without delay, belongs not only to the language of the student ready to succeed in an examination.[18] The word *prüfen* is susceptible of a double

Maria-Amata. Made up out of whole cloth, this so-called "episode" received the scathing rejection that it deserved: "*Die ganze Angelegenheit gehört ins Reich der Fama:* this whole business belongs in the realm of imaginary rumor."

16 "Sermo enim Dei facit homines a mundo recedere: it is the word of God that makes men withdraw from the world." St. Thomas, *Commentary on John's Gospel*, n. 2223.

17 A justified question as we now know, since Heidegger, who had already broken with him, did not deign to attend the funeral of his master.

18 The pastor involved, Eugene Breitling, very quickly

meaning, a proof of which is a little incident which would give the mistress of novices occasion to criticize. With respect to the *Prüfungen* (tests), Edith Stein had remarked during recreation that, in this respect, she had been well trained, and this was interpreted as a putdown of the other novices who had not like her passed many university examinations. In fact, with respect to *tests*, she thought they were something we should always spare others but from which one should never imagine oneself to be dispensed. Even before she took the habit she wrote: "I know that I must acquire the holy habit at the price of difficult testing."[19]

The suffering of others was something Edith felt more naturally when it concerned her mother and her people. Knowing that she must tell her mother something that would be unintelligible to her – that her daughter would enter Carmel – Edith undertook the trip to Breslau in order to cushion the blow with her presence when she bade her a heart-rending goodbye. It was also to spare her mother that, with respect to another bit

learned the quality of the person with whom he was to deal: "*ein Hochtalentiertes, sehr gelehrtes Fräulein Dr. phil.: A highly gifted and very learned young lady with a Ph.D.*" (ESW, VIII, p. 49.)

19   Letter to an Ursuline nun, January 26, 1934.

of news that would be difficult to bear, she advised her sister Rosa, converted in her turn to Catholicism, to let some time pass before actually receiving the sacraments of baptism and confirmation.[20] Yet these were sacraments that loomed large in their lives. There is no justification for the remark of a biographer that confirmation especially would have been a mere formality. Edith would have wanted to affirm the opposite. "Candelmas, the anniversary of my confirmation, is by that very fact one of particular importance."[21]

Nor did she forget that she herself had been the sponsor at the confirmation[22] of Miss Hermann, as she had been the godmother at baptism for another who, come from Judaism, would also end up in Auschwitz in 1942.[23] Not only did she carefully preserve her baptismal certificate, she kept as well the certificate of her confirmation. To a correspondent, she explained that she

---

20 One finds a similar scruple at this same time on the part of Henri Bergson. Converted, by the testimony and agency of Pére Sertillanges, the philosopher put off his baptism until the end of the Occupation, armed only with "the baptism of desire."

21 *Letter to an Ursuline nun*. ESW, VIII, p. 161.

22 ESW, VIII, p. 64.

23 *Ibid.*, p. 82.

could, on the occasion of this sacrament, choose a new name, if she had not already done so at baptism.[24] From Holland she sent a little Confirmation gift to another correspondent of the name of Marx.[25] She spoke of the importance of the reception of this sacrament when her sister was scheduled to receive it on Pentecost Monday 1937 at Breslau, having received her First Communion the day before at the High Mass.

Needless to say, their mother set her face firmly against these events with a categorical refusal:

> *She dismissed anything that went beyond the Jewish faith; that is why it was not possible to make comprehensible to her, no matter how minimally, the step that I had taken. She particularly rejected conversions: each one should live and die in the faith in which he was born. She had chilling images of Catholicism and of the cloistered life.[26]*

---

24 Letter to Ruth Kantorowicz, ESW, IX, p. 40.

25 *Ibid.*, p. 150.

26 Letter to Gertrud von le Fort, October 17, 1933. (ESW, VIII, p. 154.)

In Edith's eyes, this did not mean that her love of God was not authentic, any more than her love for her daughters diminished. She reproached them only for not having been sufficiently educated in the Jewish religion.[27] Both Edith and Rosa would end in Auschwitz. "We leave on behalf of our people." That simple remark at the moment when the Nazi Storm Troopers entered the door, dragged them from their convent and sent them off to the unknown, also has the force of prophecy – the intellectual expressing what her sister was going to experience along with her, the only members of their family to be victims of the Holocaust. From the time of her entry into Carmel, Edith had hoped for, and obtained, the wish that the Cross might be explicitly mentioned in the new name that would be given her. She would wear it as title of nobility: "wenn jemand den Adel 'vom Kreuz' hat: when one bears the title 'of the Cross.'"[28]

One cannot forebear thinking, by contrast, of the tomb of the two Heidegger brothers: Martin, who died first, and his young brother, Fritz, father

27 These are the points which, according to Edith, Gertrud von le Fort could depend on if she paid a visit to Breslau.

28 ESW, IX, p. 124.

of the future pastor of Sankt-Blasien in the Black Forest – Heinrich, now retired in Switzerland. Unlike his brother's, which bears a cross, the tomb of Martin Heidegger, by his express wish, bears a star, inspired no doubt by a poem of Hölderlin: "... *auf einen Stern zugehen, nur dieses! To rise to a star, that alone!*" But one might also interpret it – the mercy of the Lord being great – as a general reference to an ideal which the Scouts too sing: "a star in heaven shows us the way / let us march on, hand in hand." Or, perhaps unconsciously, as a word of the Gospel on "the profound goodness of our God, thanks to whom we are visited by a rising star, coming from on high." (Luke 1: 78)

Edith Stein herself said in a conference at Ludwigshafen in 1931:

> *The star of Bethlehem shines in a night of deep darkness. . . . The night of sin, so much more somber and menacing, separates itself from the light descending from heaven.*[29]

In any case, for her who would from now on be called Sister Teresa Benedicta of the Cross, the

---

29 *The Crib and the Cross*, p. 31.

Christian qualification of martyr does not follow from torture as such, considered in its materiality, but from the motivation of the executioner as recognized by the lived intention of the tortured who offers her life and loses it . . . *Martyrem non poena facit, sed causa: it is not the torture undergone that makes the martyr, but the cause for which he undergoes it.*[30]

"They kill the body," as the Gospel firmly puts it, and the agony of Jesus is no less comprehensible than that of his disciples. In the case of Edith and Rosa, they were put into a convoy of other religious, all of Jewish origin, which was to leave Westerbork, a staging camp, in the early hours of August 7, 1942. It was from there that Edith scribbled her last letter, dated the 6th. The transport's destination is given as uncertain, "Silesia or Czechoslovakia," followed by *two* question marks. We are struck to see her handwriting at this point deformed, unrecognizable as the beautiful script habitual to her, seemingly numbed with agony in its very firmness. She asks her superior to please send them some things, articles of toiletry, etc., but she mistook the date in writing *6.IV* instead of *6.VIII*, she mangled the word *möchte*, she broached again the idea that the

30 St. Thomas, *Commentary on the Second Epistle to Timothy* (Marietti ed.), n. 52.

Swiss, by their consulate in Amsterdam, could do something for her and her sister. The disarray is obvious.[31] Her friend Jägerschmitt (Sister Adelgundis), to whom we told these details, was so moved by them that she gave a great sigh of commiseration at the extreme distress of the prisoner just three days from her death, "The poor thing!"

Things followed their pitiless course. Departed early on the following day, the convoy arrived at Auschwitz only on August 9, and it was at Birkenau, according to research undertaken after the war, that all prisoners were executed in a gas chamber the very day of their arrival.[32]

Vinctus Christi Jesu. Thus it is that Saint Paul

31 It should be made clear that, against the biography written by Elizabeth de Mirable, the addressee of this last letter which was confided to an intermediary of good will, was not Sister Adelgundis herself (to whom I put the question), but in all likelihood, given the tenor of the content, the superior of the Dutch convent at Echt from which Edith and her sister had just been taken. Two weeks earlier, a Swiss convent (Le Pâquier, near Fribourg) had informed the monastery at Echt of its willingness to accept them. Edith thanked the superior in a letter written in French on July 24, 1942. On the efforts undertaken by Edith, at the request of her superior, to find refuge in a Carmel in Switzerland, see Philibert Secretan, *Edith Stein et la Suisse.* Ad Solem, 1997.

32 One must distinguish two camps at Auschwitz: the

describes his ultimate relation to Christ, "chained for his sake." And Saint Thomas enters into this thought: "It is most praiseworthy to be in chains for Christ: for in this way one must be made happy."[33]

Spoken perhaps with an air of youthful assurance to the pastor of Bergzabern, the *Prüfen Sie mich!* found here its fulfillment in the extreme witnessing. And to the test of this challenge, she acted indeed as a saint, recognized as such since then, as we thank God for what he has accomplished in her. No need to mention in this regard that there are unrecognized saints, as there are uncelebrated martyrs, the inevitable forgotten ones. The Church is aware of this. There is a feast, that of All Saints, that remedies with its remembrance the anonymity imposed by the contingencies of history in the mystery of the hidden

one, where the trains were unloaded, over whose entry flew the banner *Arbeit macht frei* (*Work makes one free*). It made use of old barracks, and it was there that thousands of non-Jews had been interned, abominably tortured, shot. The only "block" for Jews was to our knowledge block 20, called "the block of Jews."

33 *Commentary on Philemon* (Marietti ed., n. 4): *Laudabile enim valde est vinctum esse propter Christum; in hoc enim est beatificandus.*

God and his relation to his creatures. But when some emerge, often with visible misgivings,[34] it is a grace that is given to all.

34 At the time of her beatification in Cologne, Edith Stein would have been able to observe from on high that the stadium was far from full, only two-thirds, much less than for a football match.

THE INNER LIFE

The work of salvation takes place in obscurity and stillness. In the heart's quiet dialogue with God the living building blocks out of which the kingdom of God grows are prepared, the chosen instruments for the construction forged. The mystical stream that flows down through all centuries is no spurious tributary that has strayed from the prayer life of the church – it is its deepest life. When this mystical stream breaks through traditional forms, it does so because the Spirit that blows where it will is living in it, this Spirit that has created all traditional forms and must ever create new ones. Without him there would be no liturgy and no church. Was not the soul of the royal Psalmist a harp whose strings resounded under the gentle breath of the Holy Spirit? From the overflowing heart of the Virgin Mary blessed by God streamed the exultant hymn of the Magnificat. When the angel's mysterious word became visible reality, the prophetic Benedictus hymn unsealed the lips of the old priest Zechariah, who had been struck dumb. Whatever arose from spirit-filled hearts found expression in words and melodies and continues to be communicated from mouth to mouth. The function of the Divine Office is to see that it continues to resound from generation to generation. So the mystical stream forms the many-voiced, continually swelling hymn of praise to the triune God, the Creator, the Redeemer, and the Perfecter. Therefore, it is not a question of placing the inner prayer free of all traditional forms as 'subjective' piety in contrast to the liturgy as the 'objective' prayer of the church. All authentic prayer is prayer of the church. Through every sincere prayer something happens in the church, and it is the church itself that is praying therein, for it is the Holy Spirit living in the church that intercedes for every individual soul "with sighs too deep for words." (Romans 8: 26) This is exactly what authentic prayer is, for "no one can say 'Jesus is Lord' except by the Holy Spirit." (1 Cor. 12: 3) What could the prayer of the church be, if not great lovers giving themselves to God who is love!

The unbounded loving surrender to God and God's return gift, full and enduring union, this is the highest elevation of the heart attainable, the highest level of prayer. Souls who have attained it are truly the heart of the church, and in them lives Jesus' high priestly love. Hidden with Christ in God, they can do nothing but radiate to other hearts the divine love that fills them and so participate in the perfection of all into unity in God, which was and is Jesus' greatest desire. . . .

For those blessed souls who have entered into the unity of life in God, everything is one: rest and activity, looking and acting, silence and speaking, listening and communicating, surrendering in loving acceptance and an outpouring of love in grateful songs of praise. As long as we are still on the way – and the farther away from the goal the more intensely – we are still subject to temporal laws, and are instructed to actualize ourselves, one after another and all the members complementing each other mutually, the divine life in all its fullness. We need hours for listening silently and allowing the Word of God to act on us until it moves us to bear fruit in an offering of praise and an offering of actio. We need to have traditional forms and to participate in public and prescribed worship services so our interior life will remain vital and on the right track, and so it will find appropriate expression. There must be special places on earth for the solemn praise of God, places where this praise is formed into the greatest perfection of which humankind is capable. From such places it can ascend to heaven for the whole church and have an influence on the church's members; it can awaken the interior life in them and make them zealous for external unanimity. But it must be enlivened from within by this means; that here, too, room must be made for silent recollection. Otherwise, it will degenerate into a rigid and lifeless lip service. And protection from such dangers is provided by those homes for the interior life where souls stand before the face of God in solitude and silence in order to be quickening love in the heart of the church.

However, the key to the interior life as well as to the choirs of blessed spirits who sing the eternal Sanctus is Christ. His blood is the curtain through which we enter into the Holiest of Holies, the Divine Life. In baptism and in the sacrament of *reconciliation, his blood cleanses us of our sins, opens our eyes to eternal light, our ears to hearing God's word. It opens our lips to sing his praise, to pray in expiation, in petition, in thanksgiving, all of which are but varying forms of adoration, i.e., of the creature's homage to the Almighty and All-benevolent One. In the sacrament of confirmation, Christ's blood marks and strengthens the soldiers of Christ so that they candidly profess their allegiance. However, above all, we are made members of the Body of Christ by virtue of the sacrament in which Christ himself is present. When we partake of the sacrifice and receive Holy Communion and are nourished by the flesh and blood of Jesus, we ourselves become his flesh and blood. And only if and insofar as we are members of his Body, can his spirit quicken and govern us. "It is the Spirit that quickens members of its own body. . . . The Christian must fear nothing as much as being separated from the Body of Christ. For when separated from Christ's Body, the Christian is no longer his member, is no longer quickened by his Spirit."[1] However, we become*

1   St. Augustine, *Commentary on John*, tract 7. Edith

members of the Body of Christ, "not only through love . . . but in all reality, through becoming one with his flesh: For this is effected through the food that he has given us in order to show us his longing for us. This is why he has submerged himself in us and allowed his body to take form in us. We, then, are one, just as the body is joined to the head. . . ." As members of his Body, animated by his Spirit, we bring ourselves "through him, with him, and in him" as a sacrifice and join in the eternal hymn of thanksgiving. Therefore, after receiving the holy meal, the church permits us to say: "Satisfied by such great gifts, grant, we beseech you, Lord, that these gifts we have received be for our salvation and that we may never cease praising you." (Roman Missal)[3]

Stein read these words in the Breviary, third day of the octave of Corpus Christi.

2   St. John Chrysostom, homily 61 to the people of Antioch. Edith Stein read this too in the breviary.

3   From *The Prayer of the Church* in *The Collected Works of Edith Stein*, volume 4: *The Hidden Life*, translated by Dr. Waltraut Stein (Washington: ICS Publications, 1992), pp. 15–17.

CONVERSION FOR ALL?

As for us, exposed as we are to the downward tugs of mediocrity, it can happen that we end up rejecting concretely the idea of conversion and even more that of martyr. These are commonly thought to happen only to others. Doubtless we forget the word of the Psalmist who attributes the initiative to God: "Convert us and we will be converted."

In the example of Edith Stein, the authenticity of a conversion to the path which was for her that of life was verified and consecrated by its culmination. Like Jeanne d'Arc on her pyre, she says simply, "Jesus!" It is in this sense that must be understood inversely the term *Unglaube*, which she applied to the attitude of those, most notably the Jews, who are impeded from recognizing him "the same yesterday, today and tomorrow." (Hebrews 13: 8) What she called simply "the non-faith of the Jewish people" bears on the identity, hidden from some, revealed to others, of him who asks of each: "Who do you say that I am?"

It is not easy to identify him, and we can only do so by the Spirit working within us, showing this identify in the facts. But in how many cases the 'faith' of humans stops short of that. And so we nibble away at what still deserves the name of 'faith.' This faith Edith attributed in fact to her mother, with a shade of great admiration, while recognizing its limits: "she too has a solid faith in God."[1] But nonetheless:

> She defends herself with all her strength against my coming decision. It is hard to see the sorrow and disarray of such a mother and to have no human means of coming to her aid.[2]

Edith remained almost obsessed with this.

> The last weeks at the house as well as the separation have naturally been very painful. It was completely impossible to make anything at all understandable to my mother. She remains in complete resistance and incomprehension, and I could do nothing but go, depart, placing my firm confi-

1   Letter to Theodor Conrad, *Edith Stein, Briefe an Hedwig Conrad-Martius, op. cit*, p. 26. It is an undated letter of the summer of 1933.

2   Letter to an Ursuline nun, January 1, 1934.

> *dence in the grace of God and the power of our prayer.*[3]

Here was a test much harder to inflict – and to undergo – when all around the persecution of Jewish families intensified.

Three nephews are already in America; another is preparing to go to Palestine; only the very youngest (thirteen years old) will remain; he will be enthroned on the 23rd next in the community, as son of the Law.[4]

And, already two years earlier:

> *My family is showing patience and courage, to my great joy, my dear mother above all; she too has in fact a solid faith in God which has served as her guide throughout a long and difficult existence.*[5]

As is well known, a convent of Polish religious, Carmelites to be exact, was established fifteen years later on the border of the old concentration camp, in an undertaking of penance and prayer.

3   Letter to Hatti (Hedwig Conrad-Martius), October 31, 1933.

4   Letter to Hatti; November 17, 1935.

5   Letter to Theodor Conrad, summer of 1933.

Some Jewish authorities took offense at this, and the Catholic Church, acquiescing to their wish,[6] arranged for the transfer of this new Carmel to a site clearly separated from the camp by two streets, rows of houses, and a curtain of trees. The acquisition of this site – which was very difficult, as it involved fourteen owners – was achieved only in 1989, when Polish authorities issued permission to build.

It goes without saying that the presence of these Carmelites, who were reproached for having raised a monumental cross at the confines of the camp, had no other purpose in their own eyes than to establish a place of silence, of recollection and of prayer for the intention of *all* the victims as well as of expiation for those guilty of the most hateful crime ever committed against humanity. The Center of Information, Education, Encounter and Prayer, built in cooperation with the convent, was therefore moved, replaced by a restaurant, cafeteria, souvenir boutique, and noisy buses that offend no one (a supermarket was rightly excluded).

One can only applaud the decision of Catholics anxious not to offend the sensibility of

6   In an agreement signed at Geneva, February 22, 1987.

Jewish memories. Thus the Superior General of the Carmelites wrote to Mr. Theo Klein, former president of the European Jewish Congress, to express to him his "intention to see realized as quickly as possible" the agreement reached concerning the moving of the sisters (July 14, 1991). He added, "United with my Polish brothers and sisters [he himself is Mexican], I intend to honor with Christian fidelity the memory of the martyrs of Poland under National Socialism. That fidelity and the Catholic faith do not require that the Carmelite sister pray in the places themselves of the extermination of those martyrs."

The reply of Edith Stein *convert* gathers together the whole of her existence: her Judaism as a source, her femininity as a grace, her philosophy as a task, the last all the more important because the entire reality of the world and of mystery remains in her eyes "founded in philosophy *and* theology."[7] In that which is, for each one, "the movement of the rational creature toward God" – in the words which express the object of the Second Part of the *Summa of Theology* – the historical observer can only like a seismograph record the tremors transmitted to the surface of the expression. He registers them as best he can, kept and held to the outside of things, but he well

7   The italics are hers.

knows that, if the depths are to be sounded, it is necessary to speak in the first person and to become involved in the manner Saint Paul was. "For we have been buried with him by means of Baptism unto death, in order that, just as Christ has arisen from the dead, through the glory of the Father, so we also may walk in newness of life." (Romans 6: 4)

A crisis is always a time of discernment for souls, a kind of obligation to sort things out. Let a philosopher, a woman, a Jewess speak to us through her martyrdom.

> *The Savior turns a serious and questioning look on us and asks each of us this: Do you wish to remain faithful to the Crucified? Reflect well. The world is in flames; the open battle between Christ and Antichrist has begun. To take Christ's part may cost you your life.*[8]

That is also what Thomas Aquinas teaches when he observes that we do not always have a choice, but martyrdom may be imposed on us.

8   From a talk given at a chapter conference for the feast of the Exaltation of the Cross, September 14, 1939. In *The Crib and the Cross*, pp. 62–63.

> *There is no act covered by a counsel of per-*
> *fection that might not in some circum-*
> *stances become obligatory, as being neces-*
> *sary for salvation. Thus Augustine*
> *observes that abstinence might be required*
> *because of the absence or illness of one's*
> *spouse.*[9]

This takes nothing away from the perfection of martyrdom – or of continence – to understand that they are realities to which we ought to be disposed when they are imposed. There are instances, certainly, when Christians have volunteered for martyrdom (the case of Maximilian Kolbe is a particularly clear one, since he freely made the choice to die for one condemned in order to save his life). There was no obligation to offer himself. But there is an obligation for all to recognize the possibility of such heroism, inscribed in baptism, so that, if the time should come, the Spirit, who breathes where he wills, might bear us to it.

The highest teaching is not that which comes to us from teachers, doctors. But they could be called to a chair whose ambitions exceed their own. Doctor of the Church? It is possible that this product of the university might become that over

9   *Summa theologiae*, IIaIIae, q. 124, a. 3, ad 1m.

her dead body, so to say. Doctor of the German university? That is a title worn with much pride, at least in these parts. She did indeed teach and teach a lot, like her dear Hatti, frequent radio guest and traveler around Germany for her conferences. She was often asked to speak in those difficult times when the country advanced toward its misery – and the misery of others. Thus the word has been addressed to us "because the Holy Spirit never fails to provide for the needs of the Church, he furnishes the word," and this, as Saint Thomas explains, in a threefold way and for a threefold purpose. First, to instruct the intellect, which comes about when speech is used in such a way as to teach (*sic loquitur quod doceat*). Second, to stir feeling in such a way that, drawn to the word of God, listeners acquire a taste for it (*sic loquitur quod auditores delectet*). Finally, to prompt to act (*sic loquitur quod auditorem flectat*).[10] What difference can it then make if circumstances one day came to be such, as they were to be, when she could no longer teach? "*It shouldn't be regretted that I can no longer give lectures.*"[11] That did not stop her from remaining faithful to her vocation as philosopher and, for example, coming to the aid of a distinguished

---

10   *Summa theologiae*, IIaIIae, q. 177, a. 1.

11   Letter to Theodor Conrad, Monday after Pentecost, 1933. ESW, VIII, p. 139.

ecclesiastic whom she helped with his doctoral thesis. "A work that is certainly the result of extraordinary application, but manifestly deprived of a properly philosophical impulse."[12]

It is with reference to its end that we judge the steps of a journey, with reference to the Cross which includes Jesus that the conversion of future martyrs is gauged.

> *I have another idea of metaphysics: the grasp of the whole of reality, including revealed truth, and thus based on both philosophy and theology.*[13]

When the executioners came looking for her, demanding that Fraulein Doktor Stein be handed over to them, it was the hour when she must lift high the candelabrum, in the manner of Jesus of whom Thomas Aquinas tells us that, on the cross, he raised the light of his doctrine on its branches.

> *As a teacher bears the candelabrum in which has been put the light of his doctrine,*

12 *Ibid.*, p. 139. Then vicar of the cathedral at Speyer, Michael Habermehl, the person involved, nonetheless successfully earned his doctorate. He would be found, many long years later, assistant ecclesiastic – we would say, chaplain – of the *Bund Neudeutschland*.

13 Letter to Theodor Conrad. Edith Stein, *Briefe an Hedwig Conrad-Martius*, p. 13.

> *because the word of the cross is to the faithful the power of God.*[14]

Nonetheless, from day to day conversion does not involve much psychodrama; on the contrary it is its continuity that, in the event, remains striking. A Jewess remains a Jewess, a woman remains a woman, a philosopher remains a philosopher: all blended, as one might say of overlaid maps, the lower visible through the higher. The saint of contrasts is also the saint of constancy. Jewess, she was one to the degree that she was told that it was a bit of an exaggeration for her to speak of phenomenology as "ours," forgetting the part other non-Jewish philosophers had played in the movement.[15] Woman, she would remain interested, as the author of a "lovely blue brochure" entitled *Das Ethos der Frauenberufe* (*Ethics of the Feminine*

14 Thomas is commenting on John 19, 16–18, the account of the crucifixion. The sight of Christ bearing the cross is for the impious and unbelievers folly, but for the faithful and pious it is a great mystery. And then two analogies. Christ bears the cross as a king bears his scepter and as the teacher carries a candlestick by which his teaching illumines. "Item ut doctor portat candelabrum, in quo ponenda erat lucerna suae doctrinae, quia verbum crucis fidelibus est virtus Dei." [n. 2414].

15 The scene took place in Paris where Koyré and Edith

Professions),[16] in everything that concerned the feminist movement, to the point of counting on the fellowship of Hatti in England to help a person of the same type, similarly liberated.[17] Philosopher, as well as when she was in Carmel, where she continued without discouragement the difficult work of completing her last work – and, against wind and tide, the research of an editor.[18]

> Stein had gone in 1931 at the invitation of the Thomist Society. Visiting the capital, they noticed that their Benedictine companion, Father Freuling, was amused by the way in which, speaking of Jewish philosophers, they constantly used "we," "us," "ours," and asked them how they would classify him (he wasn't Jewish). Hatti, who reports the event, gives it an indulgent explanation. In their preferential attachment to those who were theirs, Edith Stein and Koyré (later professor at Paris and whom Edith Stein once called *der schlimme Koyré: that villain Koyré* [ESW, IX, p. 50]) were *manifesting something 'viscerally metaphysical': etwas blutmässig Metaphysisches'. Honi sout qui mal y pense* – Edith was in her way charmingly childish, according to her friend.

16 Letter of March 23, 1933. The work is to be found in ESW, V.

17 Letter of January 26, 1937. "I think that such women of the feminist movement are always happy to meet a woman able to really do something and that they are ready to help her."

18 It was not because of any lack of respect that we made

6. Conversion for All?

All that in a climate of charming ecumenism without waffling. The same comrade from Göttingen, who had asked for the times of her radio talks[19] and to whom she recommended taking advantage of studying Saint Thomas,[20] lived in the country with her husband where they farmed, both Lutherans, sent to the Carmel of Cologne an abundant supply of fruit, especially the apples that Edith had told them would be very good for the meatless diet of the religious. Selected by a sorter, the fruit arrived but with the modest dissclaimer by the sender that they were bad apples. This drew a protest from the recipient. "I am very angry that you should use such terms, armselige

some criticisms of Edith Stein as a philosopher in the book devoted to her philosophical work; quite the contrary. It must be remembered, again, that the philosopher's work was interrupted by her premature death and that her encounter with Thomas Aquinas was late. The editor of her collected works has thought it necessary to call attention to "an error of Edith Stein" in theology. [ESW, IX, p. 49], made with respect to Teresa of Avila. But he understood there what Edith Stein did not say, all the less because Sacred Scripture was for her "an incomparable treasure house." [ESW, IX, p. 41.]

19 *Wissen Sie schon die Termine Ihrer Radioverträge?* Letter to Hatti, November 13, 1932.

20 *Wenn Sie sich mit Thomas beschäftigen . . .*

Äpfel." When Christians behave in this way, ignoring confessional barriers, it is because primary for them is the love of the Lord, a sign of his presence: *ubi caritas et amor, ibi Deus est.* And that is because then, together, they are converted to the essential, that essential to which the chosen people have been invited and the nations are the heirs.

This genealogy is expressed in a simple phrase of Saint Thomas whose depth might be better manifested if put into a quatrain.

> *Ipsi Gentiles*
> *Ad fidem conversi*
> *spiritualiter Judaei*
> *Confitentes dicuntur effecti.*

> *Gentiles who choose*
> *the faith declare*
> *that now they're*
> *spiritually Jews.*[21]

In other words:

> *Even Gentiles who have converted to the faith are accounted confessing Jews spiritually, by means of a circumcision which is*

21 Saint Thomas, *Commentary on John* (Marietti ed. N. 2421).

> *that of the spirit and no longer of the flesh,*
> *so much so that the inscription "King of the*
> *Jews" on the cross signifies as well that he*
> *is the king of the converted nations.*[22]

The nobility of the Cross, to borrow a phrase from Edith Stein, is expressed by the inscription written in three languages, signifying the three levels of knowledge man is to derive from it.[23] The Hebrew marks the domination of Jesus over theology; the Greek, his mastery of natural wisdom; Latin, his power of practical philosophy symbolized by the Romans. Thus mobilized, all human knowledge is put at the service of Christ and thereby reoriented to an essential subordination: "We are destroying speculations and every lofty thing raised up against knowledge of God, and we are taking every thought captive to the obedience of Christ." (2 Corinthians 10: 5)

22   *Ibid.*, n. 2422.
23   *Ibid.*

CHRISTIAN PHILOSOPHY

Whatever proceeds from an integral view of the truths of faith and philosophical knowledge bears the mark of the double source of knowledge, and faith is an "obscure light." It gives us something to comprehend but only to indicate to us something that remains ungraspable by us. Since the ultimate depth of any being cannot be sounded, whatever is seen from this angle falls under the "obscure light," of faith and mystery, and whatever is graspable is seen in profile against an unattainable horizon. That is what Father Przywara has called the reductio ad mysterium. *We are also in agreement with him – as the above considerations indicate – when he says that philosophy is accomplished "but not as theology." On the other hand, I have trouble understanding how this union of "theology and philosophy comes about in the interior of a metaphysics." The primacy of form in theology ought certainly to be acknowledged in the sense that, with respect to the truth of theological and philosophical propositions, the last word goes to theology – in its highest meaning as the Word of God, interpreted by the magisterium of the Church. But since it is precisely philosophy, and not theology, that needs a complement to its content, it falls to it to create the unity of an englobing doctrine. So we are of the opinion that "Christian philosophy" is not only an expression of the spiritual attitude of Christian philosophers, not just the designation of teachings actually presented by Christian thinkers – the term also signifies the ideal of a* perfectum opus rationis *which collects in a synthesis everything that natural reason and revelation make accessible to us. The pursuit of this goal was concretized in the Summas of the Middle Ages; those great syntheses were the external form adequate to a universal quest. Moreover, the realization of that ideal – to include all being in its unity and in its totality – in principle escapes any human effort: already finite reality is inexhaustible and all the more so the infinite Being of God. Pure philosophy, as the science of being as being in its ultimate causes, no matter how far man's natural reason may push, in the most complete achievement imaginable, it is essentially unachieved. It is certainly open to theology and, by taking off from theology, can be completed. But theology itself is not a closed doctrine susceptible of being completed. It is deployed historically as an appropriation and progressive intellectual penetration into the revealed data of the tradition. More, it must be realized that revelation does not embrace the infinite fullness of divine truth. God communicates Himself to the human spirit according to the measure and mode corresponding to his wisdom. It depends on Him to amplify the measure. It depends on Him to give a revelation in a form adapted to human thought: to a knowledge progressing step by step to a grasp by means of concepts and judgments; or to raise man above his natural mode of thinking to a quite different manner of knowing, a participation in the divine vision which embrace everything in one look. The complete achievement of the ideal toward which philosophy tends as a search for truth is nothing else than the wisdom of God Himself, the simple vision by which God knows Himself and every created thing. The supreme realization that a created human spirit can attain – assuredly not by its own powers – is the beatific vision that God gives in uniting us to Himself, to take part in the divine knowledge while living with the divine life. The closest we can come to this supreme goal during earthy life is mystical vision. But there also exists a lower plateau, for which that supreme grace is not needed, namely, authentic vivifying faith. According to the teaching of the Church, "faith is a supernatural virtue by which, inspired and aided by divine grace, we consider as true that which God has revealed and which has been taught us by the Church, not because of the inner and real truth that we know by the light of natural reason but because of the authority of God who reveals and can neither deceive nor be deceived."* (Roman Catechism for Adults.) *Theological language designates as faith not only the virtue* (fides qua creditur) *but also what we believe, the truth revealed* (fides quae creditur) *and, lastly, the living exercise of the virtue, the act of believing* (credere), *the act of faith. It is the actual fact of believing that we have in mind now. It covers different notions: in accepting the truths of faith on the authority of God, we hold them as true and thus we have faith, or confidence, in God* (credere Deo). *But we cannot have faith in God without believing God* (credere Deum), *that is, without believing that God is God, the supreme and perfectly true being that we designate by the word God. To accept the truths of faith therefore signifies accepting God, for God is the veritable object of faith, or the subject of which the truths treat. But to accept God also means to turn toward God.[1] Thus faith is a grasp of God. And a grasp presupposes a being to be grasped: we cannot believe without grace. And grace is a participation in the divine life. If we would open ourselves to grace, if we accept the faith, we "have the beginning of life eternal in us."[2] We accept the faith on the testimony of God, and we acquire knowledge without comprehension: we cannot accept the truths of faith as evident in themselves,*

---

1   St. Thomas, *Disputed Question on Truth*, q. 14, a. 7, ad. 7.

2   *Ibid.*, q. 14, a. 2.

like the necessary truths of reason or facts of perception; nor can we deduce them logically from immediately evident truths. That is one reason faith is called an obscure light. Moreover, as credere Deum *and* credere in Deum, *it always tends beyond all the truth that has been revealed, that is, truths announced by God in concepts and judgments in the manner of human knowledge, expressed in words and phrases. Faith demands more than the particular truths announced by God, it wants God himself, who is Truth, in his entirety; it grasps him without seeing. "Although he brings the night . . ." That is the profoundest obscurity of the faith, faced with eternal clarity toward which it is oriented. It is of this double obscurity that is in question when our holy father John of the Cross writes: "The progression of intelligence is a greater anchoring in the faith; and thus to go farther means to become more obscure, since faith is obscurity for intelligence."* (Living Flame of Love). *Nevertheless, there is a progression, a surpassing of all particular conceptualizable knowledge, an access to the simple embrace of the one Truth.*

That is why faith is closer to divine wisdom

than any philosophical or even theological science. But when the journey into the shadows becomes painful, any ray of light which falls into our night as a promise of future clarity is an inestimable aid lest we go astray. And even the little light of natural reason can render appreciable service. Christian philosophy will consider as its most noble task to prepare the way for faith. That is the reason Saint Thomas had at heart to construct a pure philosophy founded on natural reason: that is the only way to go the whole way with unbelievers. If they agree to go the whole way with us this may dispose them to be led farther than was their intention at the outset. From the point of view of Christian Philosophy, there is nothing to prevent such work in common. It can draw teachings from the Greeks and the moderns, following the principle, "Examine everything and keep the best," it can keep what resists its criticisms. On the other hand, it can make available what it itself has, leaving to others the task of examining and choosing. The unbeliever has no objective reason to mistrust the results acquired by natural procedures, under the pretext that they were judged not only according to the principles of reason, but also the truths of faith. He is free to have recourse to the measure of reason in all its rigor and to refuse what appears to him insufficient. Moreover, it depends on him to pursue the road and to take knowledge of the results acquired thanks to revelation. He would not hold as "theses" the truths of faith to which one would have recourse, as the believer does, but only as "hypotheses." But to know if the consequences that one draws from them correspond or not to the truths of reason, one has a common criterion on both sides. With respect to the vision of the whole that permits the believing philosopher to encounter both reason and revelation, the unbeliever should calmly wait to see if he can agree and if he can derive some benefit from a deeper and more ample understanding of being.[3]

---

3   *Endliches und Eweges Sein*, ESW II, pp. 25–30.

CONVERSION ACHIEVED

When Edith Stein converted, she accepted what marks every conversion, that her life would be given an irreversible direction, one that might take her, following Jesus, to the witness of annihilation. A 'kenosis' that is, in the mystery of her life, the point of departure of her mounting toward God, her ascension. No doubt the lives of the saints are never recovered in their materiality, but when they unroll before our eyes it is our task to decipher them, directing our attention to the communicable cipher they can be for us. The letter Edith Stein sent from Breslau to Gertrude von le Fort,[1] another convert of the time, can speak as well to the anonymous addressees we are, avid to make a unity of Jewess, Woman, and Philosopher, reoriented from now on in their definitive axis. Listen to her speak with a disconcerting voice:

> *Your letter gave me much joy. That does me so much good in these last difficult days*

[1] Gertrud, Miss (Baroness) von le Fort was able to emigrate to Switzerland when the Nazis confiscated her goods.

*(just before entry into Carmel), when
something comes to me from people who
understood my path – opposite to the great
suffering that I had to cause here and had
every day before my eyes. You help me ask
for my mother that strength be given her
to endure our goodbye, and also that she
might be given the light to understand it.
I have often thought that it would be
important to you to meet my mother. She
bears a certain resemblance to the grand-
mother of Veronica;[2] except that she is not
a cultivated woman but has a nature completely simple and strong.[3]*

This link with her mother would never be broken.
"Throughout my life, I would have answered for
her, as would my sister Rosa who is with me in the
faith."[4]

The immovable presence of this strong
woman did not of course prevent her turning to
another interlocutor, herself a woman of character, Gertrude von le Fort.

2   A character in a novel by Gertrud von le Fort, *Das
    Schweisstuch der Veronika.*

3   ESW, VIII, p. 152.

4   Letter of November 13, 1936 to a Ursuline nun.
    ESW, IX, p. 65.

Naturally I have also thought of you during these last months, since I have known my path; it is only that from now on you are going to know Carmel truly when you come see me in Cologne. This is more beautiful than at Münster,[5] and perhaps more beautiful than at Beuron. You must not think that we have in any way lost anything. Each one who has a place in my heart and in my prayers will on the contrary gain. My beloved sisters at Cologne will heartily rejoice when you visit and you will quickly find that the grill is not a barrier.[6]

And another recurrent theme: *"I have heard of some beautiful things you have written on the essence of woman. Could I have a look at them?"*

---

5   Münster in Westphalia, which was her last teaching post before the official interdict; Beuron – it was her practice to go there for Holy Week. The Father Abbot of the monastery, Dom Raphael Walzer, known for his opposition to Nazism, took French nationality after the war in order to found in Morocco a Benedictine monastery (Tioumliline), Edith considered Beuron her second country. ESW, IX, p. 65.

6   ESW, VIII, p. 152.

The reference is to *Eternal Woman*, published by Kösel in 1934, an essay she strongly recommended a year later to her dear godmother, Hatti the philosopher, adding, *"From my first meeting with G. Le Fort, I felt a strong kinship between us."* The kinship of beings united in the search for God; kinship of the women who were there before the men on Easter morning. Their disponibility reminds us of Mary Magdalene, "this woman who by her infidelity turned her back on Christ, when converted, knew him, and turned to him." It was she who perceived someone whom at first she did not recognize but then, turning – as the Gospel text notes with precision – she did recognize the Master she sought. (John 20: 16)

The lesson to take from this episode is that in order to perceive Christ it is likely necessary to turn to the unknown and unexpected. A prophet already indicated this: "Turn to me and I will turn to you" (Zac 1: 3), as if in order truly to encounter him he is not sure that we will always know on which side he is found. The quest suffices to

---

7   ESW, IX, p. 51.

8   Thomas Aquinas: *haec mulier per infidelitatem ad Christum verterat dorsum, sed quando animum ejus ad congoscendum convertit, retrorsum conversa est. Comm. on John*, n. 2505.

engage a disponibility which will have its recompense: "Wisdom allows herself to be discovered by those who seek her." (Wisdom 6: 12)

The very fact that we have reflected on one of the witnesses of our time, in this brief sketch, however maladroit, gives Edith Stein the right to look on our lives, on our daily round. It is the gaze of a Jewess, of a woman, of a philosopher that is now illumined by the presentiment of her mission:

> *When I find myself in a profound peace –*
> *from which an abyss still separates me! – I*
> *know that then I will have a holy function*
> *to exercise on behalf of those who still*
> *remain outside.*
> > *Goodbye, in caritate Christi,*
> > *Your Edith Stein.*[9]

9   ESW, VIII, p. 153.

THE HIDDEN LIFE AND THE EPIPHANY

When the gentle light of the advent candles begins to shine in the dark days of December – a mysterious light in a mysterious darkness – it awakens in us the consoling thought that the divine light, the Holy Spirit, has never ceased to illumine the darkness of the fallen world. He has remained faithful to his creation, regardless of all the infidelity of creatures. And if the darkness would not allow itself to be penetrated by the heavenly light, there were nevertheless some places always predisposed for it to blaze.

A ray from this light fell into the hearts of our original parents even during the judgment to which they were subjected. This was an illuminating ray that awakened in them the knowledge of their guilt, an enkindling ray that made them burn with fiery remorse, purifying and cleansing, and made them sensitive to the gentle light of the star of hope, which shone for them in the words of promise of the "proto-evangelium," the original gospel.

As were the hearts of the first human

beings, so down through the ages again and again human hearts have been struck by the divine ray. Hidden from the whole world, it illuminated and irradiated them, let the hard, encrusted, misshapen matter of these hearts soften, and then with the tender hand of an artist formed them anew into the image of God. Seen by no human eye, this is how living building blocks were and are formed and brought together into a church first of all invisible. However, the visible church grows out of this invisible one in ever new, divine deeds and revelations that shed their light – ever new epiphanies. The silent working of the Holy Spirit in the depths of the soul made the patriarchs into friends of God. However, when they came to the point of allowing themselves to be used as his pliant instruments, he established them in an external visible efficacy as bearers of historical development, and awakened from among them his chosen people. Therefore Moses, too, was educated quietly and then sent as the leader and lawgiver.

Not everyone whom God uses as an instrument must be prepared in this way. People may also be instruments of God without their knowledge and even against their will, possibly even people who neither externally nor interiorly belong to the church. They would then be used like the hammer or chisel of the artist, or like a knife with which the vinedresser prunes the vines. For those who belong to the church, outer membership can also temporally precede interior, in fact can be materially significant for it (as when someone without faith is baptized and then comes to faith through public life in the church). But it finally comes down to the interior life; formation moves from the inner to the outer. The deeper a soul is bound to God, the more completely surrendered to grace, the stronger will be its influence on the form of the church. Conversely, the more an era is engulfed in the night of sin and estrangement from God, the more it needs souls united to God. And God does not permit a deficiency. The greatest figures of prophecy and sanctity step forth out of the darkest night. But for the most part the formative stream of the mystical life remains invisible. Certainly the decisive turning points in world history are substantially co-determined by souls whom no history book ever mentions. And we will only find out about those souls to whom we owe the decisive turning points in our personal lives on the day when all that is hidden is revealed.

Because hidden souls do not live in isolation, but are a part of the living nexus and have a position in a great divine order, we speak of an invisible church. Their impact and affinity can remain hidden from themselves and others for their entire earthly lives. But it is also possible for some of this to become visible in the external world. This is how it was with the persons and events intertwined in the mystery of the Incarnation. Mary and Joseph, Zacharias and Elizabeth, the shepherds and the kings, Simeon and Anna – all of these had behind them a solitary life with God and were prepared for their special tasks before they found themselves together in those awesome encounters and events and, in retrospect, could understand how the paths left behind led to this climax. Their astounded adoration in the presence of these great deeds of God is expressed in the songs of praise that have come down to us.

In the people who are gathered around

the manger, we have an analogy for the church and its development. Representatives of the old royal dynasties to whom the savior of the world was promised and representatives of faithful people constitute the relationship between the Old and the New Covenants. The kings from the faraway East indicate the Gentiles for whom salvation is to come from Judea. So here there is already "the church made up of Jews and Gentiles." The kings at the manger represent seekers from all lands and peoples. Grace led them before they ever belonged to the external church. There lived in them a pure longing for truth that did not stop at the boundaries of native doctrines and traditions. Because God is truth and because He wants to be found by those who seek Him with their whole hearts, sooner or later the star had to appear to show these wise men the way to truth. And so they now stand before the Incarnate Truth, bow down and worship it, and place their crowns at its feet, because all the treasures of the world are but a little dust compared to it.

And the kings have a special meaning for us, too. Even though we already *belonged to the external church, an interior impulse nevertheless drove us out of the circle of inherited viewpoints and conventions. We knew God, but we felt that He desired to be sought and found by us in a new way. Therefore we wanted to open ourselves and sought for a star to show us the right way. And it arose for us in the grace of vocation. We followed it and found the divine infant. He stretched out his hands for our gifts. He wanted the pure gold of a heart detached from all earthly goods; the* myrrh *of a renunciation of all the happiness of this world in exchange for participation in the life and suffering of Jesus; the* frankincense *of a will that surrenders itself and strains upward to lose itself in the divine will. In return for these gifts, the Divine Child gave us Himself.*

But this admirable exchange was not a one-time event. It fills our entire lives. After the solemn hour of bridal surrender, there followed the everyday life of observance in the Order. We had to "return to our own country." but "taking another way" and escorted by the new light that had blazed up for us at these solemn places. The new light commands us to search anew. "God lets himself be sought," says St. Augustine, "to let himself be found. He lets himself be found to be sought again." After each great hour of grace, it is as if we were but beginning now to understand our vocation. Therefore an interior need prompts us to renew our vows repeatedly. That we do so on the feast of the three kings whose pilgrimage and affirmation are for us a symbol for our lives has a deep meaning. To each authentic, heartfelt re-newal of vows, the Divine Child responds with renewed acceptance and a deeper union. And this means a new, hidden operation of grace in our souls. Perhaps it is revealed in an epiphany, the work of God becoming visible in our external behavior and activity noticed by those around us. But perhaps it also bears fruit that, though observed, conceals from all eyes the mysterious source from which its vital juices pour.

Today we live again in a time that urgently needs to be renewed at the hidden springs of God-fearing souls. Many people, too, place their last hope in these hidden springs of salvation. This is a serious warning cry: Surrender without reservation to the Lord who has called us. This is required of us so that the face of the earth may be renewed. In faithful trust, we must abandon our souls to the sovereignty of the Holy Spirit. It is not necessary that we experience the epiphany in our lives. We must live in confident certainty that what the Spirit of God secretly effects in us bears the fruits in the kingdom of God. We will see them in eternity.

So this is how we want to bring our gifts to the Lord: We place them in the hands of the Mother of God. This first Saturday is particularly dedicated to her honor, and nothing can give her most pure heart greater joy than an ever-deeper surrender to the Divine Heart. Furthermore, she will certainly have no more urgent petition for the Child in the manger than the one for holy priests and a richly blessed priestly ministry. And this is the petition today's Saturday for priests bids us make and our Holy Mother has enjoined on us so compellingly as an essential constituent of our vocation in Carmel.[1]

---

1   *The Collected Works of Edith Stein*, volume 4: *The Hidden Life*, translated by Watraut Stein (Washington: ICS Publications, 1992), pp. 109–12.

THE CANONIZATION OF EDITH STEIN

Message of John Paul II

(On Sunday, October 11, 1998, John Paul II canonized St Teresa Benedicta of the Cross, Edith Stein, a Jewish philosopher, convert to the Catholic faith, Carmelite nun, and martyr at Auschwitz. The Pope's homily follows the solemn canonization.)

> *For the honor of the Blessed Trinity, the exaltation of the Catholic Faith and the fostering of Christian life, by the authority of our Lord Jesus Christ, of the holy Apostles Peter and Paul, and our own, after due deliberation and frequent prayers for the divine assistance, and having sought the counsel of our Brother Bishops, we declare and define that Blessed Teresa Benedicta of the Cross, Edith Stein, is a saint and we enroll her among the saints, decreeing that she is to be venerated in the whole Church as one of the saints. In the name of the Father, and of the Son, and of the Holy Spirit.*

1. "Far be it from me to glory except in the Cross of our Lord Jesus Christ." (Gal 6: 14). St. Paul's words to the Galatians, which we have just heard, are well suited to the human and spiritual experience of Teresa Benedicta of the Cross, who has been solemnly enrolled among the saints today. She too can repeat with the Apostle: Far be it from me to glory except in the Cross of Our Lord Jesus Christ.

The Cross of Christ! Ever blossoming, the tree of the Cross continues to bear new fruits of salvation. This is why believers look with confidence to the Cross, drawing from its mystery the love, the courage and strength to walk faithfully in the footsteps of the crucified and risen Christ. Thus the message of the Cross has entered the hearts of so many men and women and changed their lives.

The spiritual experience of Edith Stein is an eloquent example of this extraordinary interior renewal. A young woman in search of the truth has become a saint and martyr through the silent workings of divine grace: Teresa Benedicta of the Cross, who from heaven repeats to us today all the words that marked her life: "Far be it from me to glory except in the Cross of our Lord Jesus Christ."

2. On May 1, 1987, during my pastoral visit to Germany, I had the joy of beatifying this generous witness to the faith in the city of Cologne. Today, eleven years later, here in Rome, in St. Peter's Square, I am able solemnly to present this eminent daughter of Israel and faithful daughter of the Church as a saint to the whole world.

Today, as then, we bow to the memory of Edith Stein, proclaiming the indomitable witness she bore during her life and especially by her death. Now alongside Teresa of Avila and Thérèse of Liseux, another Teresa takes her place among the host of saints who do honor to the Carmelite Order. Dear brothers and sisters who have gathered for this solemn celebration, let us give glory to God for what he has accomplished in Edith Stein.

3. I greet the many pilgrims who have come to Rome, particularly the members of the Stein family who have wanted to be with us on this joyful occasion. I also extend a cordial greeting to the representatives of the Carmelite community, which became a "second family" for Teresa Benedicta of the Cross.

I also welcome the official delegation from the Federal Republic of Germany, led by Helmut

Kohl, the outgoing Federal Chancellor, whom I greet with heartfelt respect. Moreover, I greet the representatives of the states of North Rhine-Westphalia and Rhineland-Palatinate and the Mayor of Cologne. An official delegation has also come from my country, led by Prime Minister Jerzy Buzek. I extend a cordial greeting to them.

I would particularly like to mention the pilgrims from the Dioceses of Wroclaw (Breslau), Cologne, Münster, Speyer, Krakow, and Bielsko-Zywiec, who have come with their cardinals, bishops, and pastors. They join the numerous groups of the faithful from Germany, the United States of America, and my homeland, Poland.

4. Dear brothers and sisters! Because she was Jewish, Edith Stein was taken with her sister Rosa and many other Catholic Jews from the Netherlands to the concentration camp of Auschwitz, where she died with them in the gas chambers. Today we remember them all with deep respect. A few days before her deportation, the woman religious had dismissed the question about a possible rescue: "Do not do it! Why should I be spared? Is it not right that I should gain no advantage from my Baptism? If I cannot share the lot of my brothers and sisters, my life, in a certain sense, is destroyed."

From now on, as we celebrate the memory of this new saint from year to year, we must also remember the Shoah, that cruel plan to exterminate a people, a plan to which millions of our Jewish brothers and sisters fell victim. May the Lord let his face shine upon them and grant them peace. (Cf. Nm 6: 25 ff.)

For the love of God and man, once again I raise an anguished cry. May such criminal deeds never be repeated against any ethnic group, against any race, in any corner of this world! It is a cry to everyone: to all people of goodwill; to all who believe in the Just and Eternal God; to all who know they are joined to Christ, the Word of God made man. We must all stand together; human dignity is at stake. There is only one human family. The new saint also insisted on this: "Our love of neighbor is the measure of our love of God. For Christians and not only for them no one is a 'stranger.' The love of Christ knows no borders."

5. Dear brothers and sisters! The love of Christ was the fire that inflamed the life of St. Teresa Benedicta of the Cross. Long before she realized it, she was caught by this fire. At the beginning she devoted herself to freedom. For a long time Edith Stein was a seeker. Her mind never tired of

searching, and her heart always yearned for hope. She traveled the arduous path of philosophy with passionate enthusiasm. Eventually she was rewarded: she seized the truth. Or better, she was seized by it. Then she discovered that truth had a name: Jesus Christ. From that moment on, the incarnate Word was her One and All. Looking back as a Carmelite on this period of her life, she wrote to a Benedictine nun: "Whoever seeks the truth is seeking God, whether consciously or unconsciously." Although Edith Stein had been brought up religiously by her Jewish mother, at the age of fourteen she had consciously and deliberately stopped praying. She wanted to rely exclusively on herself and was concerned to assert her freedom in making decisions about her life. At the end of a long journey, she came to the surprising realization: only those who commit themselves to the love of Christ become truly free.

This woman had to face the challenges of such a radically changing century as our own. Her experience is an example to us. The modern world boasts of the enticing door which says: Everything is permitted. It ignores the narrow gate of discernment and renunciation. I am speaking especially to you, young Christians, particularly to the many altar servers who have come to Rome these days on pilgrimage. Pay attention!

Your life is not an endless series of open doors. Listen to your heart. Do not stay on the surface, but go to the heart of things. And when the time is right, have the courage to decide. The Lord is waiting for you to put your freedom in his good hands.

6. St. Teresa Benedicta of the Cross was able to understand that the love of Christ and human freedom are intertwined, because love and truth have an intrinsic relationship. The quest for truth and its expression in love did not seem at odds to her; on the contrary she realized they call for one another.

In our time, truth is often mistaken for the opinion of the majority. In addition, there is a widespread belief that one should use the truth even against love or vice versa. But truth and love need each other. St. Teresa Benedicta is a witness to this. The "martyr for love," who gave her life for her friends, let no one surpass her in love. At the same time, with her whole being she sought the truth, of which she wrote: "No spiritual work comes into the world without great suffering. It always challenges the whole person."

St. Teresa Benedicta of the Cross says to us all: Do not accept anything as the truth if it lacks love. And do not accept anything as love which lacks truth. One without the other becomes a destructive lie.

7. Finally, the new saint teaches us that love for Christ undergoes suffering. Whoever truly loves does not stop at the prospect of suffering: he accepts communion in suffering with the one he loves.

Aware of what her Jewish origins implied, Edith Stein spoke eloquently about them. "Beneath the Cross, I understood the destiny of God's People. . . . Indeed, today I know far better what it means to be the Lord's bride under the sign of the Cross. But since it is a mystery, it can never be understood by reason alone."

The mystery of the Cross gradually enveloped her whole life, spurring her to the point of making the supreme sacrifice. As a bride of the Cross, Sister Teresa Benedicta of the Cross not only wrote profound pages on the "science of the Cross," but was thoroughly trained in the school of the Cross. Many of our contemporaries would like to silence the Cross. But nothing is more eloquent than the Cross when silenced. The true message of suffering is a lesson of love. Love makes suffering fruitful, and suffering deepens love.

Through the experience of the Cross, Edith

Stein was able to open the way to a new encounter with the God of Abraham, Isaac, and Jacob, the Father of our Lord Jesus Christ. Faith and the Cross proved inseparable to her. Having matured in the school of the Cross, she found the roots to which the tree of her own life was attached. She understood that it was very important for her "to be a daughter of the chosen people and to belong to Christ not only spiritually, but also through blood."

8. "God is spirit and those who worship him must worship in spirit and truth." (Jn 4: 24) Dear brothers and sisters, the Divine Teacher spoke these words to the Samaritan woman at Jacob's well. What he gave his chance but attentive listener we also find in the life of Edith Stein, in her "ascent of Mount Carmel." The depth of the divine mystery became perceptible to her in the silence of contemplation. Gradually, throughout her life, as she grew in the knowledge of God, worshiping him in spirit and truth, she experienced ever more clearly her specific vocation to ascend the Cross with Christ, to embrace it with serenity and trust, to love it by following in the footsteps of her beloved Spouse. Saint Teresa Benedicta of the Cross is offered to us today as a model to inspire us and a protectress to call upon.

We give thanks to God for this gift. May the new saint be an example to us in our commitment to serve freedom, in our search for the truth. May her witness constantly strengthen the bridge of mutual understanding between Jews and Christians. Saint Teresa Benedicta of the Cross, pray for us! Amen.[1]

Collect of the Mass of St. Edith Stein

God of our fathers, you led the holy Martyr Teresa Benedicta of the Cross, Edith Stein, to a knowledge of your crucified Son and called her to follow his example in death. By her prayers, bring all to recognize their Savior in the Crucified Christ and through him, to arrive at the vision of your glory. We ask this through the same Jesus Christ our Lord, who lives and reigns with you and the Holy Spirit, one God, forever and ever. Amen.

1   *Osservatore Romano.* October 14, 1998.

INDEX

Act and Potency, 63

Adelgundis, Sister (Jägerschmitt), 38, 67, 79

Amersfoort Prison Camp, 18

Angelus, 53

Antichrist, 93

Arendt, Hannah, 70

atheism of E. Stein? 55–56

Augustine, St., 86, 94, 121

Auschwitz, 18, 19, 74, 76, 79–80

Bach, J. S., 24

Baptismal Certificate, 74

BenedictineMissal (Schott) 42

Benedictus, 82

Bergson, Henri, conversion of, 74

Bergzabern, 15, 41, 43, 72

Beuron, Abbey of, 16, 112

Breitling, Eugene, 72

Breslau, 13, 24, 62, 73, 75, 110

Bridget of Sweden, St., 19

Buzek, Jerzy, 126

Calvary, xi, 62

Canonization homily, John Paul II, 123–32

Canonization of Edith Stein, 123

Carmel of Cologne, 17, 44, 56, 71, 74, 112

Catherine of Siena, St., xi, 19

Catholic funeral, 57

celibacy, 43–44

challah, 28

Christian philosophy, 102–9

Chrysostom, St. John, 87

Confirmation, 74

Conrad, Theodor, 89, 96

Conrad-Martius, Hedwig, 15, 41–43, 64, 69–70, 90, 99

conversion, 21

Culture of death, xi

Curé d'Ars, 30

Divine Office, 83

Dominicans, 15–16, 37

Duns Scotus, 64

Dutch bishops, 18

Index

Echt, ix, 17–18, 79
Edith Stein Philosopher, x, 20, 38, 44, 50, 71
Eternal Woman, 112
European Jewish Congress, 92
Exodus, 27

faith, 105–6
Fall, the, 33
Feminine question, 38
Finite and Eternal Being, 17, 63, 102–9
Frankfurt, 29
Freiburg, 16
Freuling, Father, 98
Fribourg, 29, 38, 44, 68, 70

Gaboriau, Florent, ix, x, 44, 59
Gertrude von le Fort, 75–76, 110, 113
Gifts of Holy Spirit, 59 ff.
Goethe, 30
Göttingen, 14, 20, 40, 64, 99
Graef, Hilda, 51
Günterstal, 37–38

Habermehl, Michael, 96
Heidegger, Martin, 16, 40–41, 46–49, 65–66, 68, 70–71, 76
Heidegger, Father Heinrich (nephew), 77

Heidegger, Madame, 67
Heidegger, Fritz (brother), 76
Helmut Harringa, 24
Herbstrith, Waltraud, 61
Hidden Life, the, 115–22
Himmler, Heinrich, ix
Hitler, Adolf, ix, 16
Hölderlin, 77
Holland, 75
Holocaust, 76
Hölzer, Heidi, 38
Hsiao, Paul Shih-Yi, 71
Husserl, Malville (wife), conversion, 67
Husserl, Edmund, 14–17, 31, 38, 50, 64, 66, 72

Ideas, 52
image of God, 116
Ingarden, Roman, 52, 66
Inner Life, the, 82–87
Jahrbuch, 52
Jeanne d'Arc, 88
Jews and Gentiles, 119
John Paul II, x, xi, 19
John of the Cross, St., 107
Judaism, 26
Die Jüdin, 56

Kantorowicz, Ruth, 75
Kaufman, E., 40
Kings, gifts of, 120
Klein, Theo, 92
Koeppel, Josephine, O.C.D., 25

Kohl, Helmut, 125–26
Kolbe, St. Maximilian ix, 94
Kopf, Sister Callista, O.P., 63
Koyré, 98
Krebs, Father, journal of, 69, 70

Leuven, R., 44
Lipp, Hans, 43–44
Ludwigshafen, 77
Luther, Martin, 24
magisterium, 103
Magnificat, 82
Mährisch Weisskirchen hospital, 14
Man stirbt, 47, 48, 49
martyrdom, 93
Mary and Joseph, 118
Mary Magdalene, 113
Matzoh, 26
Memories of Youth, 22–25
Meszaros, Marta, 56
A Mighty Fortress Is My God, 24–25
Moses, 116
Mother of God, 33, 122
Mount Carmel, xi
Münster, 63, 112
Mystery of Christmas, 63

Nachtmahl, 29
Nazis, 17, 110, 112
New Testament, 58

New Covenant, ix
Newman, Cardinal, 15
Neyer, Sister Mary Amata, 71, 72

Oben, Freda Mary, 35
Oblates of St. Benedict, 38
Old Testament, 58
On Death, 46–49
On the State, 15
On Truth, 63, 106
On Woman, 32–35
Ott, Hugo, 69, 71

perfectum opus rationis, 103
Pesach, 26–27
phenomenology, 63–64
Polish Carmelites, 90–92
Problem of Empathy, 14
protoevangelium, 115
Prüfen Sie mich!, 43, 72, 80
Pryzwara, Erich, 15, 102
Pseudo-Dionysius, 18
Rapallo, 38

Reichstag, 39
Reinach, Pauline ("Hatti"), 14, 30, 40, 50, 95, 98
Reinach, Adolf, 14, 40, 50, 52–53
resurrection, 58
rcvclation, 104
Roman Missal, 87
Rosenmöller, Professor B., 56

Rosh Hashanah, 26–27
Russian Front, 44

Sabbath, 55
Sacraments, 74–75, 85–86
Scheler, Max, 41, 64
Scholasticism, 64
Schwend, Canon, 15–16
Science of the Cross, 5, 18
Second World War, 44
Secretan, Philibert, x, 63, 79
Sertillanges, 74
Seyss-Inquart, ix
Shoah, 127
Simeon and Anna, 118
Speyer, 15, 16, 37, 63, 69, 96
Spiritual discernment, 59–61
Star of David, 18
Stein, Auguste (mother), 26, 75, 89, 111, 128
Stein, Dr. Waltraut (niece), 87, 122
Stein, Erna (sister), 23, 37, 51
Stein, Rosa (sister), ix, 18, 74, 111
Stein uncles and aunts, 36–37
Stein, Siegfried (father of Edith), 13, 26
Stein, Else (sister), 13

Stein, Frieda (sister), 23
Storm Troopers, 76
Summa theologiae, Second Part, 92, 94
Swiss Carmel, 18, 79
synagogue, 56

Talmudic subtleties, 55
Teresa of Avila, St., 15, 41–43, 45, 99, 125
Therese of Lisieux, St., 125
Third Reich, ix, xi
Thomas Aquinas, St., 15–16, 58, 62, 65, 69, 72, 78, 80, 93, 96–97, 100, 108, 113

Und Heidegger? 72
Unglaube, 88

Victoria School, 13

"worthless life," xi
Walzer, Abbot Raphael, 16–17, 112
Westerbork Concentration Camp, 18, 78

Yom Kippur, 26, 28

Zechariah, 82
Zecharias and Elizabeth, 118